Another book by the author:

"The Key to Freedom from Captivity"
(AuthorHouse.com)

PASTORS
ARE
PEOPLE
TOO

Harvey A. Thomas

iUniverse, Inc.
New York   Bloomington

iUniverse books may be ordered through booksellers or by contacting:

iUniverse
1663 Liberty Drive
Bloomington, IN 47403
www.iuniverse.com
1-800-Authors (1-800-288-4677)

Because of the dynamic nature of the Internet, any Web addresses or links contained in this book may have changed since publication and may no longer be valid. The views expressed in this work are solely those of the author and do not necessarily reflect the views of the publisher, and the publisher hereby disclaims any responsibility for them.

ISBN: 978-1-4502-1245-8 (sc)
ISBN: 978-1-4502-1246-5 (ebook)

Printed in the United States of America

iUniverse rev. date: 03/30/2010

DEDICATION

In MEMORY of:

Rev. Frederick Nagle
(Encouraged my becoming a
Licenced Lay Minister)

Rev. Gordon James Kirk
(Introduced, made real, and personal,
The Love of my Lord and Savior
Jesus Christ.)

Rev. Thom Black
(Recognized and Insisted on my becoming
an Ordained Minister of the
Gospel of Jesus Christ)

In HONOR of:

Rev. George Urban
Rev. Dr. Morris Alton Inch

Norma Lee - My Wife // Mark
Kenneth - My Son
(For their support in making these experiences
adventurous and meaningful.)

ABOUT THE AUTHOR

HARVEY A. THOMAS is the middle child of eleven children, born in Somerville, MA. His parents were Elmer and Cora Thomas (Now deceased). He is married to Norma Lee (Newton) since 1969. They have two children, Leslie Dionne (Stillborn) and Mark Kenneth Thomas. HIS EDUCATION was obtained by the Somerville High School ('53), Gordon College (of Theology and Missions) '54 '55, and the Berkshire Christian College (New England School of Theology) '56, '58, receiving a B.A. Degree in Theology. HIS MINISTRY to Christ (50 years as of this writing) consisted of: Chaplain for Nursing Homes and Hospitals, Jail/Prison Ministries (One-on-one 15 years), Pastor of churches in Maine, Massachusetts, Pennsylvania, and Michigan, Interim Pastor in Pennsylvania, Pulpit Supplies and Camp/Campground Pastor. HIS CREDENTIALS: Licensed/ certified Lay Minister by Union Square Baptist Church, Somerville, MA. and TABCOM (The American Baptist Churches of MA), Ordained by East Mahoning and Pine Flats Baptist Churches, ABCOPAD (American Baptist Churches of PA and Del). He became a certified C.I.S.M. (Critical Incident Stress Management) team member for Hillsdale, MI - January, 1999, after two firework factory explosions. He has worked with the Special Olympic Movement in Hillsdale, MI. He planned the worship programs for the Hillsdale Medical Care Facility in MI. He is now a member of Cambrisdge "Whos Who" Register for Professional Leaders - 2010

Preview of the Book

Writing this book made me take a close look of my life as I have lived it, to this point. It brought back many memories, some happy, some sad, some funny and some unusual. Some may consider a pastor as someone different or special than themselves, because they have been "Called" of God. Some place their pastor and family on a higher pedestal. They are considered the First Family of the church. In reality, they are no different than any member of the congregation. They simply know what God desires them to do. Everyone has a place and a job in completing the work of The Church. The pastor has the same feelings, emotions, hardships, expenses, heartaches, taxes (more than the average person) and time, as you or anyone else. They eat the same kind of food, shop at the same stores, have gone to the same schools, participate in similar activities as you and your family. They are capable of making mistakes, and errors in judgment. Perhaps as you read these pages you will be able to see yourself in similar circumstances. Jesus Christ became a human being and experienced the same things we do. The pastor is likewise human and knows what we go through in life. As such, he/she is able to assist you in your journey through life.

CONTENTS

FORWARD

 S OME of us can brush with a host of ministers during our lifetime without once realizing they are ordinary people, ordinary people called to a life's pursuit just like the rest of us; each called to one pursuit or another. Like many of us Pastor Harvey Thomas was called to service early, real early. He was drawn to a ministry in Christian service while in high school. By 1958 he held a Bachelor's Degree (BA) in theology. His mission was to follow God's Will, and is to do good work for God.

In Colossians 1:9-12, Paul tells the Apostles that he'll not cease to pray for them that they might be filled with the knowledge of His will in all wisdom and spiritual understanding. That they might be worthy of pleasing the Lord, of being fruitful in every good work and to be ever increasing in the knowledge of God, of their being strengthened with all God's might according to His glorious power, that they while serving may temper patience and longsuffering with joyfulness. Paul might as well've been talking about Pastor Harvey Thomas. He is a modern-day Apostle.

As in Job 22:23, Pastor Thomas is a unique messenger, one among thousands to sow unto men God's uprightness. Trust in God. Faith in God's word, in His promise, is of paramount importance. Faithfulness and prayer can pay bills and can provide food, shelter, and medicine for one's family. Joy is in serving Jesus Christ.

In Proverbs 9:9, we learn that by giving instruction to a wise man he will be wiser, teach a just man and he will increase in learning. Billy Graham's teachings have profoundly influenced Thomas's will to be effective while shaping a wholesome outlook on his ministry and upon life. Thomas has developed unique approaches to doing good work for God.

He compares a wedding to Christ and His church. Christ's Church consists of the believers in Christ as the Son of God. Invitations sent out represent the whosoever, the groom is Christ and the bride is the church. In his work he goes on to compare everyday events and experiences to the Bible passages in helping us to understand God's Word. In an earlier book on his jailhouse ministry he mimics Pharaoh's daughter as in Exodus 2:6. She had compassion for baby Moses even knowing he was different. We are all different, or special, he tells the prisoner, and he tells that to each of us. We are all created by God to be as God wanted each of us to be.

As to Special Olympics and camp counseling, see Romans 12:2; God turned the patient in tribulation. Or we may experience the lesson in Deuteronomy 23:5; God turned the curse into a blessing unto thee. God created each of us special, for His special purpose.

In another observation, he states that marriage is not just a civil ceremony. It is to form a triad between man, woman, and God. Also, death is not the end of life but the route to eternity. In life we make one of two choices, to spend eternity with God, or to spend eternity without God. This declaration he shares with his prisoner clientele as well as with the rest of us.

Cancer is a fear-laden term. Thomas suffered it and survival put an outlook on life and death. By God's design death is a part of life and in life we have those two choices: with God or not. Make the right choice. Believe in John 3:16. Along the way Thomas experienced the robbery of the bank where he was a teller. His advice; lay up treasures in heaven by investing in a spiritual life instead of into worldly goods that may be lost tomorrow.

Overall, learn from everyday experiences. As in James 1:5, if any of you lack wisdom, let him ask God...and it shall be given him.

Not least of all, count your blessings. See what God has done.

Ted F. Platt.
Retired Professor
Hillsdale College
Hillsdale, Michigan.

INTRODUCTION

IN this book my purpose is in no way attempting to elevate who I am as a pastor or a person of importance. In many respects I am no better or worse than any who might be reading this book. I am just one who knows that I have been honored to be called to serve God with a special Calling, to serve Him in the special role of proclaiming His Inspired Word. - The Good News of the Gospel - the Bible.

In a recent book I received; "Waiting for the Second Coming" by Ray C. Stepman, he describes a minister as a Shepherd (Chapter 2, pages 24-35). He says: "pastors are a special breed." He further states "Jesus was so human nobody would believe He was God, but we pastors are so godlike nobody thinks we are human!" He continues to say: "I am reminded that every believer is in the ministry." I am just one who has been called to minister the Word of God.

I can't help but be humbled when I review my life, in the writing of my various life experiences. I am reminded who I am and where I came from. Someone once said, "I'm not yet what I want to be, nor am I yet who I ought to be, but thank God, I'm not who I used to be..."

Many of my experiences are not too far off from what you have possibly gone through in your life. The sun shines, the clouds cover, the rain falls and the storms effect me the same way they do you.

The only possible difference I can see is that God has called us to serve Him with different ministries. We need to take time to discover what Spiritual Gifts God has given us. As the human body has many various parts (the tongue, eyes, ears, feet, heart etc) each part has a specific function for the body to function properly. The Body of Christ is also made up of various ministries to be effective. Have you discovered your unique, important ministry yet? *"Ask and it shall be given, seek and you will find, knock and it shall be opened unto you. For everyone who asks receives, and he who seeks finds, and to him who knocks it will be opened."* (Matthew 7: 7,8)

Little Taste of Heaven

Chapter One

"Let us rejoice - and shout for joy -exulting and triumphant!   Let us celebrate and ascribe to Him glory and honor, for the marriage of the Lamb [at last] has come and His bride has prepared herself. [Psalm 18:24] She has been permitted to dress in fine (radiant) linen - dazzling and white, for the fine linen is (signifies, represents) the righteousness - the upright, just and godly living [deeds, conduct] and right standing with God - of the saints (God's holy people). Then [the angel] said to me, Write this down: Blessed - happy, to the envied - are those who are summoned (invited, called) to the marriage supper of the Lamb. And he said to me [further], These are the true words - the genuine and exact declarations -of God."

Revelation 19:7-9
(Amplified)

IT was a beautiful wedding, as most weddings are, generally speaking. It was the most elaborate wedding I have ever officiated. The wedding party and guests come in from Long Island, New York. They were the Professionals, if you know what I mean - bankers, architects, developers and the likes. $1,000 was spent on the flower containers alone and imported from N.Y. to PA. They hired a Harpist, Violinist, trumpeter along with the organist. At the rehearsal dinner and the reception, we were served with the most expensive meal I have ever had (Approximately $150.00 per person.) I am not use to that kind of dining. It was a stretch-limo, Black-tie Affair. The reception lasted from 7:00 p.m. to 1:00 a.m.

Weddings have played an important role in the Life of Christ and in the establishment of His Church. It was at a wedding feast that Christ performed his first miracle during His Public Ministry (John 2:1-11). In my opinion, it was at this time the greatest advice ever given is recorded. It was not the words from the disciples or even Christ, Himself. They were words given by the mother of Christ, Mary, to the servants at this marriage feast, because they had run out of wine. She said to them: *"Whatsoever He (Christ) says, DO!"* If only the church of today would heed this advice, it would make the church's effectiveness on the community and the world more appealing.

Throughout scripture, we find that the relationship between Christ and His Church is the same as that of a Bride and a Groom. Before Christ ascended back to His throne in heaven, after His earthly ministry, He established what we know today to be the Church (A Body of Believers, aka. "the Invisible Church"). The Church is made up of believers in Christ, the Son of God (God in the flesh) and the Savior, bringing Salvation to the *"Whosoever's"* who would believe in Him, as Lord of their lives.

When we think of weddings, one of the first things to be considered is the "Guest List". Invitations are usually sent out to the desired participants. Much time and thought goes into those to be invited, as many a bride and groom can relate. Some hard feelings have resulted in some situations, until a resolution could be reached.

Christ is compared with that of the Groom, making preparation to be united with his Bride (John 14). The Church is compared to that of the Bride, awaiting the arrival of her beloved. Throughout scripture whenever the church is referred to, it is always written in the female gender. Most of the wedding plans are done by the bride, with the groom usually giving his approval. The church needs to make the necessary plans for what will truly be the Wedding of all times, that Great Union that will take place when the Groom (Christ) returns to receive His Bride (the Church). This is also known as the Rapture. This truly will be the marriage that was made in heaven.

In order for a wedding to take place a bride and groom are necessary. The beginning of creation tells us God's thoughts on this matter. *"So God created man in his own image, in the image of God created he him; male and female created he them. And God blessed them and God said unto them, Be fruitful, and multiply, and replenish the earth, and subdue it..." (Genesis 1:27,28a); "And the* LORD *God said, It is not good that man should be alone; I will make him a help mate (helper fit) for him." (Genesis 2:18)* Marriage was designed for a male and female, NOT two males or two female, according to the scriptures.

The Bride usually is the central attraction at the wedding, even though many other fine looking women may be participants in the wedding party. With this in mind, much care should be given as to whom the bride should be, by her future husband. The Book of Proverbs describes what this ideal woman should possess. Read Proverbs 31:10 -31 for the description of the *"Virtuous Woman"*. If any man is able to find one having all these qualities, he is a man of great wealth.

One of the first things a bride-to-be does is to think about what she is going to wear on this most important Day of her life. Much time and effort is spent searching for the right apparel. God gives us a little insight as the what a bride should wear. *"Let us be glad and rejoice, and give honor to him; for the marriage of the Lamb (Christ,*

4

the Bridegroom) is come, and his wife (the Church) hast made herself ready. And to her was granted that she should be arrayed in fine linen, clean and white: for the fine linen is the righteousness of saints." (Revelation 19:7,8). No one is suppose to wear white except the bride.

The invitations, mentioned earlier, to this great event have already been sent out.. They were personally delivered by the Groom, when Christ descended to earth to prepare the Way for those invited. Jesus said in John 14:6 , *"I am the way, the truth and the life, no man comes to the Father except through Me."* The invitations have been given to the *"WHOSOEVER's"* of the world. *"For God so loved the world that he gave his only begotten Son, that WHOSOEVER believes in Him should not perish but have everlasting life." (John 3:16)* Whenever we come upon the word *"Whosoever"* in scripture, you can insert your name in its place. You are the "Whosoever" that the scripture is speaking. The invitations were delivered by Christ personally, when He was crucified on the Cross of Calvary. Invitations need to be accepted and a response is necessary (R.S.V.P.) Only those who will respond will be received at the wedding. An invitation has been delivered to YOU. Have YOU responded yet?

Most weddings are a dress-up event. Some go so far as to require "Black Tie" attire. This sets the wedding guests apart from others in the surrounding area. When Christ comes for His Bride, the proper attire is also necessary. It is not a "Black Tie" that is required. The garment is white apparel, described in scripture as the "Robe of Righteousness" *(Isaiah 61:10) "I delight greatly in the LORD; my soul rejoices in my God, For he has clothed me with garments of salvation and arrayed me in a robe of righteousness, as a bridegroom adorns his head like a priest, and as a bride adorns herself with her jewels."* . The only way to obtain this robe is to be cleansed through the Blood of Christ, shed on the Cross of Calvary. They cannot be purchased by money, good intentions or good works. The price was paid in full by Christ, when He died in our place, for our sin and sinful nature. If we attempt to attend this wedding, without the proper credential or attire, sadly we will be turned aside (Matthew 7:21-23). The Church (Body of Believers) needs not to get ready, but BE READY, for we know not when the Bridegroom will arrive to receive His Bride.

A Parable found in scripture (Matthew 25:1-13) tells of ten virgins, waiting the arrival of the bridegroom. Five are not fully prepared for the wait and have not enough oil in their lamps. They find it necessary to leave, to buy oil (To get READY). The other five wise virgins are fully prepared (READY) with their lamps trimmed and eagerly waiting. When the bridegroom does arrive, only those who are READY will be received by Him (Christ).

The wedding ceremony usually is at a Special place that is meaningful to both the bride and groom. Most often in the bride's home church. This Great Event, uniting Christ to His Church, will take place in the best of all surroundings. *"And I, John, saw the holy city, New Jerusalem, coming down from God out of heaven, prepared as a bride adorned for her husband. ... And there came unto me one of the seven angels...saying Come hither, I will shew thee the bride, the Lamb's wife." (Revelation 21:2,9)*

The wedding and reception will be amidst the beauty of God's creations, seen on earth in the beautiful gardens and fountains that we only arrange, but God creates. This will be a time of true Fellowship of loved ones who arrived earlier and even those we have only heard about or read about in the scriptures. It will be a time of reflection of past events that brought us happiness and to ask questions of what life is all about, from such persons as Moses, Elijah, Isaiah, Enoch, Paul, the apostles and even from the Groom, Christ Himself. What a joy it will be to find answers to questions that have no answers here on earth.

During this time at the reception, refreshments of what is yet to come, will be served by those who are called to serve, by what we call today waitresses and waiters, but perhaps in reality are the angels, called to serve the Redeemed of the Lord.

After this time of reception, the main feast will be served. It will consist of the finest of foods, prepared by the greatest of chiefs. Foods such as: Grilled Filet Mignons with wild Mushroom Bordelaise,

Breast of Chicken stuffed with Asparagus and Sun-Dried Tomatoes, Pan Seared Salmon with Artichoke Hearts, Sun-Dried Tomatoes, and Lemon Beurre Blanc, and Mushroom Crusted Halibut with Tomato Broth, Fresh Herb Pasta and Summer Vegetables, Stuffed Shrimp, Pan Pancetta Wrapped Shrimp, to mention only a few vanities. The main Entrees will be followed with fine, delicious desserts: Caramelized Bananas, Chocolate Terrine, Lemon Parfait, and Chocolate Covered Strawberries and Prickly Pear Sorbet in a Lemon Cup.(This was the menu for the wedding reception I attended.)

If you think this is something worth living for, wait until you see what God has prepared for the Union of Christ and His Church. Man can only provide a sampling of the best we have to offer, God prepares the Best, to perfection. The amount of food is unlimited, because with our new Resurrected Bodies. calories and fat content will not be of any concern. We will be able to eat what we desire, whenever we desire. Time will be of no concern because where this wedding will take place time does not matter or exist. *(II Peter 3:8). "Dear friends there is one thing you must not forget. With the Lord one day is like a thousand years and a thousand years is like a day."*

The crowning moment of this great event will be when the Bride (the Church) and the Groom (Jesus Christ) are presented to all of heaven and the Union of the Two become a final reality. The witnesses will greatly rejoice even though they cannot fully appreciate what the Bride has experienced, salvation from eternal condemnation. The music will be beyond our belief, as the harps, violins and trumpets and all other instruments, play the music that will crown this Great Event. Even those who feel they can't carry a tune, will be able to sing melodious tones of praise This will most definitely be a marriage that was designed in heaven.

When we all get to heaven, What a day of rejoicing that will be!
When we all see Jesus, we'll sing and shout the victory.

What I have learned by this experience?:

As we journey through life, we find we have had good experiences, bad experiences, adventurous experiences, disappointing experiences, exciting experiences, hurtful experiences, and many, many others that we could mention. This has been a good experience for my wife and I. Of all the weddings I have officiated, this was by no means the most interesting.

There is a marriage made in heaven we should consider. The Bride is the Church that was established by Jesus Christ after His Resurrection. The Bride-groom is Jesus Christ, Himself, described as the Lamb of God. To explain what I have learned, let us think back into the Old Testament times and see how weddings took place back then:

To attend any wedding it is necessary to receive an Invitation to the event. Such an invitation has been delivered to one and all, who will attend. It is located in the Word of God, the Bible (Revelation 19:7-10)

"Let us be glad and rejoice and give Him glory, for the marriage of the Lamb has come, and His wife has made herself ready. "And to her it was granted to be arrayed in fine linen, clean and bright, for the fine linen is the righteous acts of the saints. "Then he said to me, "write: 'Blessed are those who are called to the marriage supper of the Lamb!'" And he said to me, "These are the true sayings of God. "And I fell at his feet to worship him, But he said to me, "See that you do not do that! I am your fellow servant, and of your brethren who have the testimony of Jesus. Worship God! For the testimony of Jesus is the spirit of prophecy."

The three steps of the Old Testament Marriage ceremony are:

1. The Betrothal - Marriage contract. (Equivalent to our present day Engagement)

— It was arranged by the parents years before the event happened. The marriage between Christ and The Church

was arrainged by The Heavenly Father before the Church was organnized at Pentecost
— This was a time for the two to get to know each other and to grow together.
— When a person accepts Christ as Savior, they enter into a similar arrangement.
— This allows for a growing relationship between the person and Christ.
— It give one a chance for maturing in the faith.

2. When things are ready the Groom comes to receive His Bride.

— She is escorted to the home that was prepared for them (John 14)
— The Rapture of the Church - Meeting Christ in the Air (At any moment)
— The giving and receiving of Gifts. (The Five Crowns)

3. The Wedding Feast

— Celebration of the Union of Christ and His Church
— The Bride's body is changed into the Resurrection body – Like unto the Groom's

God doesn't call the qualified
He qualifies the Called.

The
Right
Combination

Chapter Two

"I will hope continually, and will praise You yet more and more. My mouth shall tell of Your righteous acts and of Your deeds of salvation all the day, for their number is more than I know."

Psalm 71:14,15
(Amplified)

T HE other day my family and I traveled to Pennsylvania for a wedding of our grand-niece. When we arrived at my Mother-in-law's home, we settled in for the week-end. As we prepared for our first night at about 10:00 p.m, I went into the bedroom to open the suitcase for my wife. It was one of those suitcases that didn't have a key, only a combination. You set the combination before you shut the case and lock it. We very seldom locked it because it was always with us. The combination was made of a three digit number. Once you have set the combination, you need to set the combination before trying to open it. We chose to use 0-0-0, because it was easy enough to remember. We didn't have to turn the dial at all.

This night, I tried to open the suitcase and nothing happened. I checked the combination dial and it was set at 0-0-0. My first thought was that somehow the dial got moved before closing the case for our trip. I thought, "Now, what am I going to do? It must have a new combination." My wife got, not only excited, but panicked. She wanted the case opened, (right NOW). All of our bed things were in the case. She was quite upset to say the least. She said, "Break it open if you have to. I need the night clothes." I wasn't about to ruin a good piece of luggage until it was necessary.

I knew I had to find the right combination, if at all possible. I turned the dial to 0-0-0 once again but nothing happened. I had no choice but to start at the beginning, 0-0-1, 0-0-2, 0-0-3, 0-0-4, etc, and so on until I reached 1-0-0, tying to open it after each and every number. I then turn it back to 0-0-0 once again with high expectation. Your right, nothing happened. By this time my wife was more than upset, if you can imagine what I mean. She said once again, "Break it open, I need what's inside NOW." I told her we might have to go to bed in our under garments for the night and work on it in the morning". She didn't really go for that imaginative suggestion. It simply was not an acceptable idea. I prayed that God would come through for me.

I continued once again 1-0-1, 1-0-2, 1-0-3, 1-0-4 etc, stopping at the hundred mark once again to try 0-0-0. You guessed it, nilz. By this time my son came into the room, trying to please his mother, saying. "It's 0-0-0 dad." as if I didn't know. I continued on with my tired mission all the way to 9-9-9   Once again I tried, 0-0-0, again with no effect. I prayed once again, "God, You know what the combination is. Please help me to find it." By this time my wife finally was willing to accept my previous suggestion. I wanted to wait until tomorrow when my two brothers-in-law we around to help if they could.

I decided to stop and go watch T.V. to settle myself down. That didn't work either. I decided to bring the suitcase into the living room to work with it while I watched T.V. I placed the case before me once again, praying silently. I noticed the medal piece by the combination dial. There was a line in the medal running vertically. I said to myself, "Self, what do you suppose would happen if I tried to pull this apart?" I did just that and would you believe the suitcase opened. I brought the open case to my wife and what a sigh of relief came across her face. She wasn't about to close the case again all the while we were there. She expected we would have to go buy new clothes the next day. God came through once again.

Isn't this much like what our lives exemplify? We put within our lives all the "things" we deem important and necessary, until we are filled to capacity. We get so much "Stuff" in our lives we have to rent storage units to keep it. We don't have enough time to use it. When we try to open, to get what we really need, we find we have lost the combination. We try and try until we are ready to "give up" or "through in the towel". We then turn to God and say, "What can I do?" "I don't have the answer."

Only when we settle down, become "still", can we discover that God has the right combination and is ready to give it to us, if only we would ask Him. *"...ask now, and you will receive, that your joy may be overflowing." (John 16:24b - Phllips). "You don't get what you want because you don't ask God for it. (James 4:3a, Phillips).*

You need to stop struggling, stop trying to do things your way. Jesus Christ said, *"I am the WAY, the TRUTH, and the LIFE...."* Turn your controls over to Him. He'll unlock the secret combination for you. He will empty out the "Stuff" in your life that's holding you back and will fill the void with nothing but blessings, that only He can give.

What Have I learned by this experience ?

As we travel through this life we call "Humanity", we find ourselves in situations we would rather not be in. We sort of feel as though we are held captive by our circumstances, not always of our own making. We know there is a way out, we just don't know which way we should turn. If only we could know the future, we would know the right combination of deeds that would be useful for all concerned. Try as we might, we often times fail in our endeavor. What's one to do when we find ourselves in this predicament?

There is a Key that will unlock the door of wisdom. In my book, written earlier,"The Key to Freedom From Captivity", we discover that the "Key" is the One and only Jesus Christ. He said in the Bible (His Written Word) *"I am the Way, he Truth, and the Life. No one comes to the Father except through Me. (John 14:6) "Casting the whole of your cares - all your anxieties, all your worries, all your concerns, once and for all - on Him; for He cares for you affectionately, and cares about you watchfully [Psalm 55:23]"* (I Peter 5:7 - Amplified)

Patrick M. Morley in his book "The Man in the Mirror" says something very significant for our consideration at this point: "Life is a big question mark. God is the big answer. Whatever the question, He is the answer. No matter how down or up, tired or strong, befriended or betrayed, upright or dishonest, hurt or happy, rich or broke, successful or failed, famous or unknown: God is the answer - He is all we need." (Page 318, Chapter twenty–four "How Can a Man Change?")

Don't put a question mark (?) where God has put a period.

The
Lock - Up

Chapter Three

"Let your character or moral disposition be free from love of money- [including] greed, avarice, lust and craving for earthly possessions - and be satisfied with your present [circumstances and with what you have]; for He (God) himself has said, I will not in any way fail you, nor give you up, nor leave you without support. [I will] not, [I will] not, [I will] not in any degree leave you helpless, nor forsake nor let [you] down, [relax My hold on you] - Assuredly not! [Joshua 1:5]"

Hebrews 13:5
(Amplified)

ONE day I went to the county jail on my regular visit. After signing in, I knew I was going to have to wait. This is normal when one goes to visit inmates. The sheriff walked by a number of times and saw me waiting. This time he let me in, himself and escorted me to the cell area. He brought me to the "turn-key", a guard monitoring the inmates, whose name was John. The Sheriff said to John, "Here is a good man whose doing a good work for us. You make sure he gets the best bunk in the facility." Friends like that, who need enemies? There's nothing like being appreciated, but I think this is going a little too far.

I was called on another occasion by John, to come and talk with a juvenile who he thought needed some one to talk with. He was asked if he wanted to talk with a pastor and he said he did. The young man, 15 years of age, was placed in a cell by himself. It was known as the incorrigible cell, where troublesome inmates were isolated from the population. This being an adult facility, he had to be by himself until they could transfer him to a juvenile, lock-up facility.

John allowed me to go into the cell with this young man. He locked us inside together, as this young man wasn't suppose to be seen by anyone. After spending about an hour or so, I was hoping John would come by and let me out. We continued to talk about life, spiritual things and the likes. Soon the hour turned into two and no John. I tried to get someone's attention via the camera, but with no results. Now it soon became three hours, then four. It was now time for the shift to change. No one but John knew I was there and he was going to be leaving for the day. We prayed that somehow John would show up. God always answers prayers for His children. Shortly thereafter, John did show up. He apologized. He had gotten so busy with his regular duties, he completely forgot I was there. As he was leaving he finally remembered me. I never did let him forget the time he locked me up. Now we can look back at it being a humorous experience and we laugh about it today. As a result of this, a new ruling was instituted at the jail, no one but inmates are allowed in the cells for any reason.

If the truth be known, we all find ourselves locked up with unfortunate situations, and circumstances, where we see no way out, no escape as it were. The inmates have tried on their own, to find escapes from such circumstances, such as using alcohol, drugs, illicit sex, etc, and they ended up becoming incarcerated in the county jail or state correctional facilities.

Let us never forget to remember that there is always One who knows where we are at all times. God said, *" 'I will in no wise fail you, neither will I in any wise forsake you' We, therefore, can confidently say: 'The Lord is my helper; I will not fear: What shall man do unto me?'"* *(Hebrews 13:5 Phillips)*

If we want to find our freedom and leave our place of confinement, we need to take time to come to Christ and learn how to "be still" and LISTEN to the voice of God speak to us. Christ is at the door of our heart, knocking and waiting for us to respond, to open the door to our hearts. There is no door latch on the outside of that door. It can only be opened by us, on the inside. We will never hear that knock as long as we are busy doing our things, our way. Only when we're "still" and quiet will we be able to hear Christ knocking. If we will simply open the door to our heart and receive Him (Christ) by letting Him into our lives, will He come in and sup with us. *" See, I stand knocking at the door. If anyone listens to my voice and opens the door, I will go into his house (your heart) and dine with him, and he with me. As for the victorious, I will give him the honor of sitting beside me on my throne, just as I myself have won the victory and have taken my seat beside my Father on his throne. Let the listener hear what the Spirit says.."* *(Revelation 3:20-22 Phillips)*

What Have I learned by this experience?

No one enjoys, looks forward to, desires, or anticipates being separated from family, and/or loved ones. We were created to function together with others and not to be isolated, an island unto ourselves. We limit our potential when we try to go it alone in this world. We need the assistance of the abilities, wisdom and experiences of others, especially those who are older and have already gone through what we find ourselves going through. No one likes being told what to do or when to do it, but we can learn how to travel our journey through life more easily and enjoyably, that makes our lives more productive and meaningful, not only for us but for those around us.

Sometimes we have to make the most of our situations and find the good in them. When the Apostle Paul wrote to the churches he started these words : *"...I have learned how to be content (satisfied to the point where I am not disturbed or disquieted) in whatever state I am. I know how to be abased and live humbly in straitened circumstances, and I know also how to enjoy plenty and live in abundance. I have learned in any and all circumstances, the secret of facing every situation, whether well-fed or going hungry, having a sufficiency and to spare or going without and being in want. I have strength for all things in Christ, Who empowers me - I am ready for anything and equal to anything through Him, Who infuses inner strength into me, (that is, I am self-sufficient in Christ's sufficiency)." (Philippians 4:11-13 - Amplified).*

We don't change God's Message - His Message changes us.

Pay - Day

Some Day

Chapter Four

"My God will liberally supply (fill to the full) your every need according to His riches in glory in Christ Jesus."

Philippians 4:19
(Amplified)

"Now unto Him that is able to do exceeding abundantly above all that we ask or think, according to the power that works in us. Unto him be glory in the church by Christ Jesus through out all ages, world without end."

Ephesians 3:20,21

W HEN God called me into Full-time Christian Service as a high school student, I had no idea how this could possibly happen. I come from a family of 11 children, being the only one from the family to receive a high school diploma. The funds needed simply weren't there for higher education for anyone in the family. I knew I would have to rely on God completely, if this was going to happen.

After graduating from high school, I prayed that God would make it possible for a college to accept me, seeing I did no take college subjects while in high school. I knew if I did enter college, it had to be God's will, not mine. I was accepted by Gordon College of Theology and Missions in Boston, Massachusetts. I attended there for two years until they relocated. I then transferred to the New England School of Theology for three years. Upon completion I received a Bachelor's Degree in Theology in 1958.

During my first year at Gordon, I received a bill from the college that needed to be paid immediately without any means of doing so. I turned it over to God in prayer, reminding Him (As if He needed to be reminded) of my financial need. I mentioned this need to no one but God. A few days later I picked up my mail. An envelope was in my mail slot with a note enclosed saying, "We felt led to give you a small gift." It was signed "Friends". To this day I still do not know who put it there. Then again I really do know. It had to be God, who else? Inside the envelope there was the exact sum of cash, equal to the amount I needed to pay off my debt to the college.

While serving God in my first pastorate in Pennsylvania, which was a yoke ministry, (that is serving two churches at the same time.) my cash salary was $7,000 a year. I know it wasn't much, but I was finally where God wanted me to be, in the pulpit proclaiming God's Word. With this I had to pay for the utilities for the parsonage. They thought they were doing us a favor by providing a parsonage as part of the package. In reality, the pastor has to pay social security tax on the fair rental value of the parsonage. It sure is amazing how quickly the bills come in before you have the means to pay them. The bills just seem to get bigger and bigger.

One day I received a telephone call from New York, where my insurance company, that carried my medical and retirement accounts, is located. They told me they knew of my financial situation and asked me to give them the totals of my indebtedness. Within a week or two, I received a check in the mail for over $1,500, so I could get rid of all my indebtedness. They told me this was a grant and I didn't need to worry about paying them back .

A year or two later my car decided to give me some problems. The transmission needed to be replaced. They didn't take credit cards, so I would have to pay cash when it was ready. I began to rob Peter to pay Paul, as the saying goes. By the time the car got fixed, I still lacked a bit. I didn't know what I was going to do. The next day as I opened the mail, there was a check from someone in town made out for the exact amount I needed to get the car. I thought that was really something. Don't you agree? The rest of the story, as Paul Harvey would say, is that I received another call from New York. Yes, once again from my insurance company. They told me that they had heard of my car trouble. They asked for the total of the bill. I hesitated to tell them but I felt I had to. Again within a week or so, I received a check (grant) for the total amount of the bill to repair my car. In the end I not only got the car repaired, but I had additional money to boot. What do you think about the God I am serving? Most times we get more than what we deserve.

The last three years of my second pastorate in Pennsylvania were somewhat difficult, especially the last year. Without going into the specifics, I ministered to the church a full year without a pay-check. My wages for preaching that year was the privilege of living in the parsonage. It was a most difficult year to experience. My son had some physical problems in school which hospitalized him at the cost of $1,000 per day for a prognoses of 10 weeks, without any medical insurance. I didn't know what to do. I finally had to go the state for medical assistance. While applying for medical help, the man I was speaking to suggested that I go to the federal social security and apply for SSI for my son. I did and he did qualify for assistance, which also covered his medical bills completely.

During that same year, a pastor friend of ours, who worked a farm along with pastoring, stopped by and asked if we could use some meat. One can always find use for hamburg. He proceeded to bring in box after box. He delivered in full, half of a cow. All kinds of cuts. Our freezer was full to capacity. Today he has received his reward for faithful service as he stands in the presence of his Creator.

Also during this year, we were sent a Love Check from one of the local churches who became aware of our plight. Not one check but a monthly check. Thank God for churches who know what it really means to serve God. When my wife and I went shopping for food in the local super market, when we returned to our car we discovered an envelope on the driver's seat. Inside the envelope we found a sum of money left by someone. God only knows who. The reality of that is, it was God who supplied when there was a need. Throughout that year, without a paycheck, I found myself making double car payments each month, while I had the money to do it, in case there would be one month I couldn't. That month never showed up.

Not done yet! I moved to Michigan in February. Before we left PA my family and I received as Christmas Gifts, the total sum of over $4,000. I ended up leaving the area with more than when I started. This only goes to prove what an awesome God we serve. How can anyone doubt the existence of God? Someone once put it this way: "God's work, done God's way, will never lack God's supply". The words of scripture puts it this way: *"My God will supply all that you need (not want) from his glorious resources in Christ Jesus. And may glory be to our God and our Father forever and ever, amen!" (Philippians 4:19,20 - Phillips translation)* All God asks of us is that we use whatever resources are at our disposal. Whatever we are lacking He will provide, so that we will be successful in all we do for Him. .

What have I learned by this experience?

Some churches have the idea that they need to hold on to their reserves for rainy days. They take only the interest the bank pays to help in their expenses. They come to God asking that He will provide the necessay funds to operate. (*"Give us this day our daily bread... "*). How can we ask for more when we haven't used what He has already porvided?

I have been told on numerous occasions that a person should be worthy of his hire. That simply means, when a person does a job or task, he/she should be paid accordingly. Sometimes it may seem not appropriate or enough. The value of any possession or deed is in the view of the one who is receiving it. The value of a collector's coin, stamp or painting is only worth what one can get for it, or what the market allows. We don't always get what we think we are worth. Maybe what we need to do is make our worth more valuable to others.

"For the kingdom of heaven is like a landowner who went out early in the morning to hire laborers for his vineyard. Now when he had agreed with the laborers for a denarius a day, he sent them into his vineyard. And he went out about the third hour and saw others standing idle in the marketplace, and said to them 'You also go into the vineyard, and whatever is right I will give you' And they went. Again he went out about the sixth and the ninth hour, and did likewise. And about the eleventh hour he went out and found others standing idle, and said to them. 'Why have you been standing here idle all day?' They said to him 'Because no one hired us.' He said to them, 'You also go into the vineyard and whatever is right you will receive.' so when evening had come, the owner of the vineyard said to his steward, 'Call the laborers and give them their wages, beginning with the last to the first.' And when those came who were hired about the eleventh hour, they each received a denarius. But when the first came, they supposed that they would receive more; and they likewise received each a denarius. And when they had received it, they murmured against the landowner,, saying, 'These last men have worked only one hour, and you made them equal to us who have borne the burden and the heat of the day.' But he answered one of them and said, 'Friend, I am doing you no wrong. Did you not agree with me for a denarius? Take what is yours and go your way. I wish to give to this last man the same as to you. Is it not lawful for me do what I wish with my own things.? Or is your eye evil because I am

good?' So the last will be first, and the first last. For many are called, but few are chosen.'"

Matthew 20:1-16

Suffering from truth decay?
Brush up with your Bible

The
Triad
Union

Chapter Five

"For as a young man marries a virgin [O Jerusalem], so shall your sons marry you; And as the bride-groom rejoices over the bride, so shall your God rejoice over you."

Isaiah 62:5
(Amplified)

TODAY marriage has wandered away from its original definition and intended purpose. To many, marriage is nothing more than legalized pleasure between a man and a woman. Some have gone so far as to try to legalize same-sex marriages, with only the physical pleasure in mind. I read in a book, recently, that in the 70's there were more divorce applications than there were marriage licenses granted by the government.

The reality of marriage needs to be more than the union of two people, as many believe it is. A successful marriage must be a triad (a threesome union - the Bride, the Bride-groom and God). God is to be the cement that holds the marriage together when times of difficulty arise (and they will most certainly). I heard also not too long ago, that the wedding party must consist of 19 people - the Bride, the Bride-groom, the Minister, four better, four worse, four richer and four poorer. (Sorry about that!)

The places I have used to marry couples have varied by the desires of those getting married. Some weddings have been performed by the lakeside, others have taken place in private homes, public buildings, country clubs and back yards. Most marriages have been performed in a church, which I prefer. I usually ask why they desire a church wedding over a civil marriage, that can be performed by most people with authority. The usual reply is that they would like to have God's blessing on the marriage. This usually opens the door for me to talk about their relationship with God, before they get joined together in wedlock. I have also been asked to officiate at weddings in a prison setting. I don't believe this to be a proper setting for such a holy ceremony and so I have not done any. I read recently of a marriage that was on top of a rock. The rock used was the Rock of Gibraltar, in St. Michael's Cave. When asked why, the groom replied, "We chose this site because we wanted to found our marriage on a rock." (#3317 - Encyclopedia of Illustrations). Another wedding took place where the bride and bridegroom were handcuffed to each other during the ceremony. It happened in Cambridge, Massachusetts. They were tipped off before hand that some friends planned to abduct the bride at the wedding. The groom fooled them. He fixed it so they'd have to abduct him also.(#3318 E.I.) The increasing divorce rate is rapidly making America 'the land of the free'. A visiting Englishman acidly observed. Yes, admitted his American companion, but remember the marriage rate is increasing too. That shows America is still 'the home of the brave.'" (#3335 E.I.)

I find it quite amusing to observe the various types of people that are attracted each other. They say that opposites attract. Some have been an introvert to an extravert, one over six feet tall to one who is only four feet tall, people of different race backgrounds, a youth to one of greater age, one neat in appearance to one more casual, one of higher education to a laborer, one with and one without money, etc. It only goes to prove that physical appearance is not the main quality that makes a successful marriage. The main factor that I search for when counseling a couple is their expression of Love for each other, (without coaxing by me). I take great pleasure in recalling the marriages I have performed. In my file, I not only keep a copy of the license and forms I have provided for information, but also pictures of each of the couples. Some I may never meet again, but it sure is good to relive their happy event. In 1971, the groom (105 years of age) married his bride (70 years of age). (#3299E.I.) The oldest bridegroom on record was one of 115 years of age from the Dominican Republic on vacation to a 16 year old, 99 years his junior. (#3300 E.I.)

Marriage is more than a piece of paper that legalizes the union by the state. According to what God wrote in His Word, the Bible, marriage is to be taken seriously. Long before there were states and governments, God established the union of two people, as a form of life, which we call marriage today. It was affirmed by Jesus Christ, as He attended a wedding in Cana of Galilee. (John 2:1-11). It was here that Christ performed His first miracle, the turning of water into the best wine of the event. It was also here at this event the "Greatest advise" was given, not by Christ, as one might assume, but by His mother, Mary. She turned to the servants and said to them, *"Whatsoever He says, DO IT!"* The same advice is applicable to all who desire to follow in the steps of our Savior, Jesus Christ.

Marriage is important because when two people who truly love each other and become as one, the Family Unit is developed. The family is said to be the backbone of the nation. As the family goes, so goes the nation. Satan is busily at work destroying the Family Unit by all means we make available to him.

Living together, without marriage, seems to be the trend of today, and children are being conceived in such unions. We hear a lot about illegitimate children, but there are no such people. All we have is illegitimate parents. This is why many youths end up living against the law of the land. They have no one to look up to as role models. Some don't even know what it means to be in love. They have never been told that they are loved, or the product of love. The ones I have spoken with, who are incarcerated, would love nothing better than to hear, "I Love You" from their parents, especially from their fathers.

"Those who God has joined together, let no man put asunder."

Have you ever heard of the "Biblical Math"? It is nothing like algebra or trigonometry. It is simply arithmetic. You don't need a college degree to understand.

God is the One who is solely interested in *"addition"*. Nowhere in scripture can I find where God or Christ subtracts from anyone's life. I do find however, where Christ states in the Gospel of John: *"I have come that you might have life and that you might have it more abundantly." (John 10:10)*

If there is to be any *"subtracting"*, it will have to be done by you or me. After receiving Christ as our Savior and being indwelt with the Holy Spirit, we discover we're uneasy with certain things in our lives that are contrary with our Christian Walk. We decide to remove (subtract) them, because they are only negatives that work against the life we are searching. The subtracting is done by us not God.

Satan is the one who delights in doing the *"division"*. He runs to and fro, seeking those things he can devour (divide.) With his help and that of his agents (the fallen angels, known as demons) we find where they have divided families, relationships, friendships, governments and even the Christians Churches, that end up being split over minute and insignificant differences that have little or no importance in the Mission of the Church. Beware of Satan at work in your times of difficulty.

"Multiplication" is the work for all whom God created on earth, namely man, animals of all kinds and even plant life. *"Be fruitful and multiply."* is the command given by the triune God - the Father, the Son and the Holy Spirit. This is done by means of procreation. Most all things that are reproduced is accomplished through multiplication rather than one for one. Note the number of kernels on an ear of corn that comes from one single kernel that is planted, the number of peas in the pods and beans in string beans which come from one single

bean being planted. The number of acorns and pine cones that come from a tree, the result of a single seed planted, etc, etc, etc,

The marriage of one man and one woman usually produces more than one child (in most cases) into a household. The single cell in the human body is replaced on a regular basis. I have read where every cell in the human body is replaced every seven years.

What have I learned by these experiences?

Marriage was never designed to be just a civil ceremony, allowed and controlled by the government. It is meant to be a holy union between one man and one woman, so designed to share intimate love toward each other and to reproduce offsprings to replenish the earth.

To most, marriage is a union between two people who like what they see and feel and desire to have a pleasurable relationship throughout life. The reality is that it must become a triad (Threesome), the coming together of three, The Bride, the Groom and Almighty God. Marriage was never meant to be just a physical relationship between two people but a Spiritual Union with God at the center. God takes what the two can offer biologically, and mysteriously, miraculously creates another human being to replenish the earth.

The first miracle Christ performed was at a Wedding in Cana in Galilee, where He turned water into wine when it ran out. Not just any wine but was is described as the best wine. You might say that He put His stamp of approval upon this ceremony, which man so often takes lightly.

Man's way leads to a hopeless end. God's way leads to an endless hope.

The

Curtain

Closes

Chapter Six

"If Christ lives in you, [then although your natural] body is dead by reason of sin and guilt, the spirit is alive because of [the] righteousness [that He imputes to you]. And if the Spirit of Him Who raised up Jesus from the dead dwells in you, [then] He who raised up Christ Jesus from the dead will also restore to life your mortal (short-lived, perishable) bodies through His Spirit who dwells in you."

Romans 8:10-11
(Amplified)

DEATH is the one thing that man tries to avoid at any cost. They don't want to think about it, let alone talk about it. They try to shy away from preparing for it for themselves or their loved ones that are near this earthly final event. One reason for this is because it is one of those great unknown's in life. If we can't see what is ahead, we just don't want to go there. To some death is nothing more than the end of life. They are buried in the ground and that is all there is. Others may think about heaven but can't see themselves good enough to go there. Some think all they have to do is get out of life all that life has to offer and they go for the gusto.

The reality is that death is a part of life. We begin to die the moment we are born. If I read scripture correctly, I believe we were created by God to live forever. We were created to have fellowship with Him. Because of disobedience, man fell from grace and become a sinner, breaking that fellowship. We were created for His pleasure not ours.

The length of one's life on earth is not up to us. God has a Plan for each of us and knows just how long we have to fulfill that Plan. The only thing that hastens one's death is if we take it away from ourselves, even then God is fully aware of that as well. Death is God's prerogative not man's. Some are taken at birth, as was our daughter, Leslee Dion Thomas. Others are taken as youths, adults and some live to be quite mature, even over one hundred years, as was my mother-in-law, who went to her heavenly abode at the age of 101. Death is a natural part of life as I have mentioned earlier, but it is caused by various diseases such as AIDS, Cancer, Diabetes and heart attacks. Some are a result of accidents, others by murder and some die simply because of old age.

How one handles death, when it comes our way, is largely dependant upon our relationship with our Creator, God Almighty. The word I like to use to describe death, seeing none of us have ever experienced it, is "separation". When we die physically, we are separated from our bodies, separated from all of our loved ones, separated from all of our earthly possessions and separated from the world as we know it.

You may not want to believe it, but we were created to live forever. There is nothing we can do to stop it, even if we wanted to. We are all going to die a physical death. *"For the wages of sin is death." (Romans 5:23). "It is appointed unto man once to die, then comes the judgment." (Hebrews 9:27).* Even though we are going to die, physically, we are going to live forever, spiritually. Not only is there a physical, there is a second death. Using the same definition that I used earlier, when we die the second death (Spiritual death) we will be "separated" from God for all eternity. Yes, we are going to live forever, but where we will spend eternity is our choice, no one else's. God is Holy and we were born with a sinful nature and the two cannot co-exist. God is still desirous of having fellowship with His creations (man - humankind), so He provided a Way for us to be restored and to have our sin forgiven. He came to earth in the form of a man (Jesus Christ) and lived a perfect human life. He did this in order that He might die our death, caused by our sin. Though born a "sinner", we can become a "saint" (a Child of God - part of His Family). *"He that has the Son has Life, he that does not have the Son does not have Life" (I John 5:12).*

I have conducted many a funeral during my ministry. My first was when I was a Lay-minister in Massachusetts. Just before the service was to begin, the funeral home lost it power supply. I had to conduct a Candle-light funeral service. It was a unique experience for me. My most difficult funerals is when I have to conduct funerals for children and young people. I feel they have been taken before their time. That's just my feeling.. I also find it difficult to take part in family member's funerals, of which I have had many. I feel uneasy when called upon to have funerals for people I have never met or those I don't know what their relationship with God may be, not knowing where they will be spending eternity.

I do enjoy the funerals of those I know to be brothers or sisters in Christ. This is not a time for mourning only. It is a Celebration of Life. A greater life then we can possibly imagine. Christ has gone before us to prepare a place for us, so we can be where He resides in the life hereafter (John 14:1-6).

My daughter, who I mentioned earlier, has gone to be with Christ some 38 years ago, as of this writing. We chose not to see her in death. We are looking forward to seeing her, face to face at that great re-union. We have never seen her, but be assured we will recognize her on that glorious day.

My suggestion to you is to make your way to the church of your choice while you can, to make preparation for that day when you will face death personally. Don't wait until six strong men carry you there, when you won't be able to make that choice. Discover now, God's Love for you while you still can. He is waiting to receive you as His child. Jesus Christ said, *"I have come that you might have life and that you might have it more abundantly" (John 10:10)*

Not too long ago, death came knocking at the door of my family. I first was told that the sister-in-law of two of my sisters had passed on, while also being told that my brother was in a comma and my sister was in intensive care. A few days later I was informed that my oldest brother, George, had died without regaining consciousness. I made arrangements to fly back east to have his funeral at the National Cemetery on Cape Cod, MA. I flew back home days later only to receive the news that my Sister Ivy, who was in Intensive Care, had gone to her heavenly abode. (I did get to see and talk with her days earlier, on her birthday.) I did not return for her funeral because of finances and I did get to see her while she was alive. The day before her funeral I received a call that the mother-in-law of my youngest sister, in Missouri had passed on,

As tragic as this was for the family, God did fulfil His promise that He would use this for good, for those who were His. *"We know that all things work together for good to those who love God, to those who are the called according to His purpose." Romans 8:28 NKJ.*

I finally got to meet the children from my brother George's first marriage. I hadn't seen them in over 40 years, since the divorce. I not only saw the children, but also their children and grand-children. A sadful event was turned into a great reunion.

What have I learned by this experience?

Death is not the end of life. It s just the beginning of a New Life in Eternity. How we will spend eternity will depend largely on how we are living life here on earth. No one really knows how long we have to live on earth . Death (separation or departure from earth) is only a breath away. Some people die early in life and some live as long as my mother-in-law, Gertrude Mae (Studebaker) Newton, who died at the age of 101.

I had the unfortunate privilege to conduct the funeral services of two young men. One I had as a camper at our denominational camp at Lake Louise in Michigan. While in high school, he was driving home after shopping for a Father's Day gift and was hit by another vehicle and he and a friend died. The second was a young man who had turned his life over to Christ while incarcerated for some stupid behavior. While he was riding home in the back of a pick-up (which no one should ever do), he was thrown from the vehicle and was killed instantly. Had these young men not received Christ as their Savior, they would not be in the presence of Christ today. You see it's not a matter of GETTING READY when the end of life on earth arrives, it is a matter of BEING READY. There may not be time to GET READY. Time is of the essence. Do not delay in making YOUR decision concerning Christ. *"For He (God) says: 'In an acceptable time I have heard you, And in the day of salvation I have helped you' Behold, NOW is the accepted time; behold NOW is the day of salvation."*   *(2 Corinthians 6:2 - N.K.J.)*

Some may have the opportunity to work for Christ early in their life, while others may not begin their work until late in life. Does this mean that those who started early should be rewarded greater than those who started later? The answer is NO! God owes no one anything. (Matthew 20:1-16 - Page 30) Those who started early, have more opportunity to receive the blessings for a longer period of time than those who started late. Those who work for God should "count their blessings" more than rewards for service. The longer we have opportunity to serve God, the richer our lives become. Let us be thankful for the time we have to work for Him. Others will have little or no time to enjoy serving Him as their Lord and Master.

Give God what's Right

not what's Left.

The Victory Lap

Chapter Seven

"The Lord lives; blessed be my rock, and exalted be God, the rock of my salvation. ...For this I will give thanks and extol You, O Lord, among the nations; I will sing praises to Your name."

2 Samuel 22:47,50
(Amplified)

T HERE are many words in our vocabulary that we like to shy away from, simply because of their negative connotations that have a way of depressing us and even scaring us. Some of these words are: failure, funeral, death, accident, hospital, surgery, divorce, etc. We all have words we keep away from using whenever possible. The one word I didn't want to hear, and the physicians tend to avoid using is the big "C" word - "Cancer." There's just something about that word that sends chills up and down one's back.

I changed my doctor about 10 years ago. One of the first things, he required was that I have a complete Blood-work done, to update my medical file. You name it and I am sure it was tested. Part of this testing was the P.S.A. I didn't even know what it meant and the fact that it only effected men. P.S.A. is the abbreviation for the medical term Phosphatic Specific Antigen. To show my medical ignorance, I didn't even know what the prostate was let alone its function. It is unfortunate that we do not get involved in matters of importance until they effect where it hurts most, ourselves personally or members of our family.

When the results of the testing came, my doctor told me I had an enlarged prostate, which in itself is nothing to be overly concerned about. This can come about by an infection or benign growth. This is not uncommon for men over the age of 50. I learned that the acceptable range for the P.S.A..is between 0 and 4.0. My testing revealed I had the count of 4.3. He proceeded to give me the physical exam, using his finger, if you know what I mean. He felt some polyps, which were of great concern to him. He referred me to an urologist in Coldwater. Believe it or not, the doctor's name was Dr. Wu. (Remember Richard Dawson and Johnny Carson's made-up doctor on the tonight Show and Family Feud.?). After examining me and feeling the growths, he suggested that I get a biopsy.

I went to the hospital, had the biopsy and waited for the results. Shortly thereafter the results came in and it showed that the growths were malignant. He made sure he didn't use the big "C" word (Cancer). He proceeded to give me five options: 1. External radiation (a treatment every day for about 6 weeks at a local hospital), 2. Freezing (the area involved would be frozen so it would not spread), 3. Implanted seeds (Radioactive seeds implanted in the prostate), 4. Implanted Isotopes (Neutrons implanted in the effected area), and 5. Surgery (the cutting out of the prostate completely). After reading up on these, along with many prayers for God's intervention, I decided to have the surgery. I asked the doctor before surgery to recheck and make sure, in case God did perform a miracle After all, via the talents He gave to man. God hadn't, for reasons only He knew, so the doctor proceeded with the surgery. The end result is that I have been free of cancer ever since, going on twelve years now (as of this writing).

This makes me a Cancer Survivor. As such, I began to participate in the American Cancer's "Relay for Life" Walk, held each year, in Hillsdale, in the later part of May or early June. This is a 24 hour (Friday, 6:00 p.m. through Saturday 6:00 p.m.)walk. The participants walk around the track all this time, for however long they wish, in order to raise money for cancer research. Because the students at Hillsdale College are in recess at this time, they decided to have a "Relay for Life" of their own for the college students. This is the third year they have done this. I have taken part the last two years.

During the "Relay for Life" the Cancer Survivors walk the first lap, which has come to be called the "Survivors" Lap. Those taking part receive a special T-shirt, along with a medal to wear and a small luncheon is provided. Being a Survivor for twelve years now, I would like to take this opportunity to encourage ALL MEN over the age of 40 to go and have their doctor prescribe a P.S.A. test. It doesn't hurt and only takes a few minutes of your time. I didn't have any symptoms of cancer. Had it gone undetected I probably would have inoperable cancer. It really is not optional as much as it is a matter of life or death. If there is a problem, the sooner it is discovered the better the results.Time is of the essence. If not for yourself, do it for your family.

About a month after I was diagnosed with my cancer, I called my two-year older brother, Willis, and encouraged him to have his prostate checked. He did so and discovered that he, like me, had prostate cancer. His PSA was much higher than mine. After having a biopsy it was determined that his cancer was inoperable. All they could do for him was to treat the cancer with medication, which proved to be quite costly, even after the insurance company paid their share. For the last twelve years his cancer was in remission, so long as he took the medication.

I was informed a few months ago that his PSA was risen to over 200 (0 - 4 is the acceptable range). He had to begin having external radiation treatments (about 8 total) every day. My sister-in-law informed me, with these new treatments it costs over $2,500 monthly. Their insurance covers only one month's expense. Last report all was going well with him

This goes to teach us the importance of checking out our health early and often. I do believe in Divine Healing, but God has given some the special ability to heal the human body. I also believe we should avail ourselves of the wisdom He has given to others. As we keep our material houses in good repair, we need to keep our physical house in good shape also. It is better to be safe now than sorry later. Don't you agree? Cancer can be deadly if ignored. If it is discovered early, it can be treated effectively and even add years to our lives. The key is to discover as early as possible what needs attention. New and better treatments are being found daily.

What have I learned by this experience?

Death needs to be considered more than just something that is the absent of life. In reality it is part of life. Death was not part of God's Design when He created the earth and all that is in it. Death came as a result of the Fall of man in the Garden of Eden. *"The wages of sin is death...." (Romans 6:23) "just as through one man sin entered the world, and death through sin, and thus death spread to all men because all sinned - " (Romans 5:12)*

Good metaphors to describe death is: a doorway through which one passes from a physical life to an eternal life, a commencement, where one begins a new life, a place of employment where one is promoted to better benefits. Life on earth is only temporary, whereas Eternal Life is a life without an end.

Exercise daily,
Walk with the Lord

Here Today
Gone Tomorrow

Chapter Eight

Community Baptist Church

"Do not gather and heap up and store for yourselves treasures on earth, where moth and rust and worm consume and destroy, and where thieves break through and steal; but gather and heap up and store for yourselves treasures in heaven, where neither moth nor rust nor worm consume and destroy, and where thieves do not break through and steal; For where your treasure is, there will your heart be also."

Matthew 6:19-21
(Amplified)

ONE of the many secular jobs I have had before entering the full-time Ministry was that of being a bank-teller in one of the banks in Massachusetts. One of the things I learned as a bank-teller is the great responsibility that goes along with the job. When you stop to consider the amount of money that goes through the hands of a bank-teller, you can sympathize with them for the low wages they receive, for such great responsibility. They are accountable for every penny that is passed between the teller and the customer. We have heard that some people (especially the teenagers) believe that money must grow on trees. We know that banks have all kinds of money to deal with. All the banks I know have branches. Branches are there to produce fruit, right?

Not too many years ago, a movie was produced entitled "Good Cops - Bad Cops". It depicted a bank robbery wherein some local cops were involved in the robbery . The essence of the film is based on a real robbery that took place in the state of Massachusetts around the late 1970's. I know it was based on fact, because I was employed at one of the branches of that bank that had been robbed.

It took place during one of the long, four-day week-ends. It was not discovered until Tuesday of the following week. It took twenty-four hours to get into the vault from the top side, so I was told. It took another twenty-hours inside the vault to open over 700 safe-deposit-boxes. What a mess it made when discovered. When the vault was opened that Tuesday morning, the local, metropolitan and state police were notified, along with the F.B.I. The robbery took place in the main branch and I was working in one of the branches. A special room was set up, at the main branch, and all the employees were asked to come and help with the inventory of the opened boxes,. Guards were all around, while we did the inventory.

We were instructed to write down everything we found in the boxes, one by one. The depositors of the boxes were notified and asked to bring in the inventory they had of what was inside their boxes. The two inventories were then compared, so that they only received back what was on their inventory, if anything. You can be sure the I.R.S. were not far behind, to see what was hidden and not reported. I am confident that not all contents were reported at that time, for obvious reasons. The contents no doubt were hidden for some reason. These items are not insured by the bank.

We were instructed to take our time as we made the inventory. All papers, regardless of their size or contents were to be looked at, to gain their importance. I came across a crumbled-up napkin in one of the boxes. I started to discard it as waste, but remembered our instructions. As I opened the napkin I discovered a three caret diamond gem. Upon further search I came across an appraisal for the gem. It was appraised for over $75,000. I sure took a sigh of relief, knowing what I almost had done. I turned it over to one of those in authority.

A variety of other items were found in the open boxes. One of the boxes was filled to the very top with nothing but loose change. It had to be someone's "Piggy Bank". Where else should it be but in a bank? Of course, there had to be a counting of all the loose coins. Another one of the boxes was filled with nothing but $100 bills, totaling over $50,000. I discovered where the term "Filthy Money" comes from. My hands were truly filthy after handling all that money. A number of the boxes had all kinds of savings bonds connected with other countries. A note was found in one of the boxes that read, "Give the contents of this box to my son (and his name appeared)." The only thing in the box was the note. Someone put directions as to where valuable items could be found within the home. I guess they didn't trust the bank completely. Documents of all kinds were also found. On the floor, about ankle deep, were hundreds of silver dollars. How or who would decide who got what silver dollar and how many of each would be given, I'm not sure it was ever decided.

After all was said and done, and before I ceased my employment with the bank, I was told that over $15 million was stolen. According to the papers it was reported to be the largest bank heist in the country at that time. The amount stolen may never really be known. I am sure not all was reported that had been stolen.

Nothing that is in safety-deposit-boxes is insured by the bank, because there was no way of knowing what was in the boxes. If they were insured, it had to be done by the owner of the contents of the boxes by their insurance companies. It was also reported that there were some "Bad Cops" involved with the robbery, thus title of the motions picture "Good Cop - Bad Cop". It was also reported that some of these cops involved were found dead, shortly thereafter.

What was the lesson to be learned by this experience?

What treasures are laid up today, may very well be lost tomorrow. Scripture tells it this way: *"Don't pile up treasures on earth, where moth and rust can spoil them and thieves can break in and steal. But keep our treasure in Heaven where there is neither moth nor rust to spoil it and nobody can break in and steal. For wherever your treasure is, you may be certain that your heart will be there too." (Matthew 6:19,20 - Phillips translations).*

In the Encyclopedia of Illustrations I found this article, "From their unfortunate experiences with robberies, the large Bank of America compiled interesting statistics about crimes and criminals. They found an average bank robbery netted $1,900 and 85 percent of thieves were caught and convicted. Robbers received an average fifteen-years in federal prison for their crimes, which meant they made only $125 per year for their dangerous endeavor. This figure is even further reduced with the recovery of the stolen money. It is easy to conclude that bank robbery is not a very profitable occupation, although there does not seem to be a shortage of personnel." (C.R. Hembree) #5987.E.I.

I recently read in an article that the amount of money spent by Americans on Storage Units to store away the STUFF they don't have room enough in their homes is $17 Billion, which is now larger than the motion picture industry. Think for a moment how much money you would have to use, if you didn't spend it on STUFF that you really didn't need. I suppose you would just spend it today on STUFF that would appear to be on sale. One of my fellow-writers who enjoys writing poetry, wrote the following poem dealing with STUFF:

COLLECTOR

Why does one collect stuff?
Is it a hoarder in disguise?
Is there ever enough?
When does such a person get wise?

Stuff's a detached back-pack,
To carry ev'rywhere we go.
What we own is in the pack,
Weighing down our life's journey so.

We unpack from a trip,
Re-establishing who we are.
It helps steer our ship
Grounds us, and to see things afar.

Clutter matters greatly;
It incarcerates our freedom
To think clearly, freely,
Incapacitates wisdom.

Our first step is stopping
The flow of imparting the stuff
Then, it is exporting
Like a cold: Enough is enough!

Let's sort to have less:
It's worth it, you'll feel more alive.
The secret to success...
One task at a time, to survive.

molly a marsh
6 September 2005
5:11 A.M.

Every fall I start stirring my stuff. There is closet stuff, drawer stuff, attic stuff and basement stuff. I separate the good stuff from the bad suff, then I stuff the bad stuff anywhere the stuff is not too crowded until I decide if I will need the bad stuff.

When the Lord calls me home, my children will want the good stuff, but the bad stuff, wherever there is room among all the other stuf, will be stuffed in bags and taken to the dump where all the other people's stuff has been taken.

Whenever we have company they always bring bags and bags of stuff. When I visit my son, he always moves his stuff so I will have room for my stuff. My daughter-in-law always clears a drawer of her stuff so I have room for my stuff. Their stuff and my stuff... it would be so much easier to use their stuff and leave my stuff at home, with the rest of my stuff.

This fall I had an exra closet built soI would have a place for all the stuff too good to throw away and too bad to keep with my good stuff. You may not have this problem, but I seem to spend a lot of time with stuff...food stuff, cleaning stuff, medicine stuff, clothes stuff and outside stuff. Whatever would life be like if we didn't have this stuff?

Now there is all that stuff we use to make us smell better than we do. There is stuff to make our hair look good, stuff to hold us in and stuff to fill us out. There is stuff to read, stuff to play with, stuff to entertain us and stuff to eat. We stuff ourselves with food stuff.

Well, our lives are filled with stuff. Good stuff, bad stuff, little stuff, big stuff, useful stuff, junky stuff, and everyone's stuff. Now when we leave all our stuff and go to heaven, whatever happens to our stuff won't matter. We will still have good stuff God has prepared forus in heaven.

-- author unknown.

What have I learned by this experience?

Many people spend too much time, money energy, effort, obtaining what they think they need to exist. They can't let anyone get more than they have. They are not satisfied with keeping up with the Joneses, they want to pass them. They go out of their way trying to provide for their children the things they had to do without while growing up. We have so much STUFF (material things) that we have to hire places to store it.

What we spend so much time obtaining can all disappear overnight. There is no safe place to hide things in today's world, not even Safety Deposit Boxes in a bank. It is far better to lay up treasures in heaven (Investing in the spiritual lives of others), safe in arms of Jesus.

WARNING!
Exposure to the Son
May prevent burning.

Eleven -

- Eleven -

- Eleven

Chapter Nine

Built - 1899

Present Structure

"Train up a child in the way he should go, and when he is old he will not depart from it."

Proverbs 22:8
N.I.V.

Oₙₑ of the major parts of a Church Program is that of the Youth Ministry. After all, the future of the church is found in its youth. Many of the larger churches have someone to run the youth program. Most of the smaller churches depend largely on adult volunteers to help the youth of the church and the community in their spiritual and social development.

The various denominations sponsor a Youth Fellowship of some kind. A number of these are called B.Y.F, M.Y.F and the likes (Baptist Youth Fellowship and Methodist Youth Fellowship etc.) One of the more popular and recent programs is called "OWANA", consisting of Bible Memorization, social activities, badges and ranks of various types. Some church sponsor Cub, Boy and Girl Scout Troops.

I grew up in a church that had as their youth program a Christian Endeavor Society. This is a non-denominational Organization. It consists of local societies, including county and state gatherings. It grew to even becoming an international organization. It began in 1881 at the Williston Church in Portland, Maine. Its founder was Dr. Francis E. Clark, D.D., LL.D., receiving his degrees from Dartmouth College in 1873 and Andover Newton Theological Seminary in 1876..

By 1883, the movement had spread across America with the first junior C.E. society being established in the Fist Congregational Church in Berkeley, California In 1886 it soon became international with societies being found in South Africa, India, Turkey , Spain, Australia, Samoa, Mexico, Chile, Brazil, Egypt, Belgium, Russia, Denmark , Norway, Korea and many others. Dr. Clark retired from active leadership and was succeeded by Dr. Poling.

The most unusual feature of the Christian Endeavor meetings is the fact that they are run stickly by the young people, themselves. No adult ever stands in front of the group, except when the officers are installed and then only as a speaker, not as one who is presiding. The primary purpose of interested young people, in themselves and in the church, is still the principal aim and endeavor.

In the local society of the church I grew up in, the youth met weekly, usually on a Sunday evenings. The youth mainly ran the meeting consisting of talks, singing of choruses, Bible studies and games. At various times during the year (sometimes monthly) various activities were held, such as hay-rides, home singsperations, and what was called Progressive suppers (the youth group would travel to various homes and at each, be served a portion of a complete meal. One home would serve a salad, another soup, another vegetable, another meat and another dessert). It was a lot of fun and fellowship. Quarterly, we would meet with other societies in the county to have fellowship and share our Christian experiences and talents. Once a year in Massachusetts, we would gather with the youth from various parts of the state for what become known as the "11-11-11 Climb".

This was held in the north-central part of Massachusetts, where we would gather on the 11th day of the 11th month , at the 11th hour to climb Mount Monadnock. Some years it was great weather, other years we had to put up with cold, wet, and/or snowy weather. It really didn't matter. It was a fun time for all who participated. In the late afternoon we would meet in a nearby church for a meal or just hot chocolate and goodies.

On the first Sunday in February we would celebrate what came to be known as Youth Sunday. This was when the youth of the church took over the entire worship service. Various young people would take the different parts of the service, such as one would lead the singing, and others would take the offering, reading the scripture, leading in prayer and one delivering the sermon. This is how I got my start into becoming a full-time pastor.

On one of these Youth Sundays I was in charge. I had used an object lesson. From a piece of plywood I had made a large "C" with the letter "E" within. Holes were drilled into the middle of each letter and I had wired large Christmas lights (red and white) into each hole and plugged it in. During the service I had asked the congregation for personal testimonies. As each testimony was given, I would light up each light in order, hoping enough testimonies would be given to light the entire sign. It went over very well.

An interesting story is told in Billy Graham's book entitled "Angels" (page 134-135) showing how the angel's messages usually have a note of urgency:

"We can illustrate this from the sinking of the Titanic. The greatest ship of its day, weighing 46,000 tons, it was considered unsinkable. But on the night of 14 April 1912, while moving through the ocean at 22 knots, it struck an iceberg. Because it carried only half as many life jackets as passengers when it sank 1,513 people drowned. Even though this event occurred more than 70 (now over 90) years ago, there is still a great fascination about it. The recent discovery of the hulk of the titanic has revived our interest in the whole tragic story

"Out of tragedy, however, God can still bring triumph.

"One passenger, John Harper, was on his way to preach at Moody Church in Chicago. Trying to stay afloat in the ocean he drifted toward a young man holding onto a plank. Harper asked, 'Young man, are you saved?' the man said, 'No.' A wave separated them. After a few minutes they drifted within speaking distance of each other, and again Harper called to him, 'Have you made your peace with God?' The young man said, "Not yet.' A wave overwhelmed John Harper and he was seen no more, but the words,'Are you saved?'' kept ringing in the young man's ears.

"Two weeks later a youth stood up in a Christian Endeavor meeting in New York, told his story and said, 'I am John Harper's last convert."

What have I learned by this experience?

One of the things I have learned is the importance of becoming involved with other young people (and people in general). We were not created to live an isolated life. We learn from our peers and we also learn by making mistakes (If we don't learn anything by our mistakes, what is the sense of making them?).

By participating in the 11-11-11 Climb, I came to appreciate the awesomeness of our God. As I stood atop Mount Monadnock and gazed into the state of Vermont, New Hampshire and Massachusetts, I could see the magnificence and majesty of God's Creative Power. Nature as I look upon it, could not just happen without a Master of divine ability behind its creation. As I stood gazing at the newly fallen snow in the wintery weather, the trees with its various colors in the Fall weather and the sun shining on the land in the summer, "I stand amazed" in the presence of an almighty God.

Be ye fishers of men
You catch them -
He'll clean them.

Here Am I
Lord,
Send me!

Chapter Ten

"I heard the voice of the Lord saying: 'Whom shall I send, and who will for Us?' Then I said, 'Here am I! Send me.'"

Isaiah 6:8

Mᴙ first encounter with the Billy Graham Evangelistic Association came while I was attending high school in Somerville Massachusetts in 1953, when there was a Crusade in the Boston Gardens, the former home court for the Boston Celtics. If my memory serves me right, I attended the Crusade meetings nightly, traveling via the bus and elevated train services.

I don't remember a time in my life when I was not interested in anything that was related to Christ and His Church. My mother (truly dedicated to her family) made it a point to send my siblings and me off to church, even though she, nor my father, attended on a regular basis. The best way anyone can give their children the proper spiritual development is not to send them to church but to BRING them to church. A proper example is of greater value to children then having them hear, "Do as I say, not as I do".

There's something about the preaching of Billy Graham, the music of the combined crusade choir, the singing of George Beverly Shea and Ethel Waters that just captivates an audience. One's feelings are very hard to describe in words. You have to be there to feel the working of the Holy Spirit in a gathering of thousands of people.

It was during this time that I was seeking seriously the leading of God, as to where my life would be heading. You see, while I was a junior in high school, I attended a state convention of the Christian Endeavor Societies (mentioned earlier). It was held for a week on the campus of the Northfield School for Girls, during the summer break. This school, along with the Mount Herman School for Boys was founded by the late Dwight L Moody, one of the great past evangelists.. He also founded the Moody Bible Institute in Chicago Illinois. At the closing service of this C.E. Convention at Sage Chapel, I dedicated my life to serve Christ, wherever it might lead. The service was concluded by the congregation singing the familiar hymn, "Living For Jesus, A Life that is true". While singing, we exited the chapel with this prayer, (the chorus of the hymn) I will never forget:

"O Jesus, Lord and Savior, I give myself to Thee,
For Thou, in Thy atonement, Didst give Thyself for me;
I own no other Master, My heart shall be Thy throne,
My life I give, henceforth to live, O Christ, for Thee alone."

My first experience with the Billy Graham Crusade was truly inspirational to say the least. You might say it laid the foundation for my future full-time service to God.

It would take another fifteen years before another Crusade would be held in Boston at the former Boston Gardens. It was held during the week of September 18-26, 1964. I have complied a booklet, containing all the news articles printed in the various newspapers throughout New England and in the Decision Magazine (December, 1964 issue).

This time, I not only attended the meetings but got throughly involved in the Crusade. The preparation for the Crusades begin usually a year in advance. It takes that much time to form the various committees needed for fund-raising the event, arranging for the location, intensive prayer preparation, assembling the choir from various churches, publicity and the training of the counselors to assist the enquirers each and every night. I read in one of the Decision Magazines that at one of the Crusades, the person in charge of preparing for the Crusade was named Harvey Thomas, but not yours truly.

At this Boston Crusade, I chose to become one of the Counselors. We had to meet many times at Tremont Temple (A Baptist church right in Boston). We were instructed there as to what to expect, given the material that would be handing out and how to go about using said material. The material packet contained a copy of the Gospel of John, a letter written by Billy Graham, two units of a Bible Study to be sent to the Billy Graham Association when completed and a place to sign a decision card if one chose to receive Jesus Christ as their Personal Savior. We had to become familiar with the various verses of scripture that should be used. These were called the "Steps of Commitment":

1. The FACT of Sin - Romans 3:23

   "For all have sinned and fall short of the glory of God,"

2. CONDITION of the sinner - Acts 26:18

   "To open their eyes and to turn them from darkness to light, and from the power of Satan to God, that they may receive forgiveness of sin, and an inheritance among those who are sanctified by faith in Me."

3. The PENALTY for sin - Romans 5:12

   "Therefore, just as through one man sin entered the world, and death through sin, and thus death spread to all men, because all sinned."

4. The penalty MUST be paid - Hebrews 9:27,28a

"And as it is appointed for man to die once, but after this the judgment, so Christ was offered once to bear the sins of many."

5. The penalty PAID by Christ - Romans 5:8

"But God demonstrates His own love toward us, in that while we were still sinners, Christ died for us."

6. Salvation is a FREE gift - Ephesians 2:8,9

"For by grace you have been saved through faith, and that not of yourselves it is the gift of God, not of works, lest anyone should boast."

7. We must RECEIVE Christ - John 1:12,13

"But as many as received Him (Jesus) to them He gave the right to become children of God, even to those who believe in His name;"

8. ASSURANCE of Salvation - I John 5:12,13

"He who has the Son has life; he who does not have the Son of God does not have life. These things I have written to you who believe in the name of the Son of God, that you may KNOW that you have eternal life, and that you may continue to believe in the name of the Son of God."

I was also given the task of assigning the pastors and counselors places throughout the Boston Garden, where the meetings were to be held. You might say it felt good to tell other pastors where to go (In a good way that is.)

When the Crusade finally began in 1964, each and every meeting was filled to capacity and an overflow crowd was located elsewhere within the building, listening on close circuit T.V. Near the close of the Crusade, it was reported that 197,545 people attended the Garden along with the overflow. It was also reported that some 8,631 enquirers made decisions to allow Christ to become part of their lives.

At the end of the meetings each night the pastors and counselors would come forward, along with the enquirers. After a few words from Billy Graham, the counselors/pastors would talk with the enquirers in small groups or individually, about the reason for their coming forward. The packet of material would be given to them and an explanation of the verses dealing with salvation, an opportunity would then be given to them to decide what they wanted to do about Christ. During the week of the Crusade, I personally talked with twenty-four (24) individuals, some of which I still have contact. There's no greater joy one can experience than to lead another person to Christ and see them accept Christ as Savior. I remember talking with one young man who was a student at M.I.T (Massachusetts Institute of Technology). He listened patiently to what I had to say, but decided he didn't want to make a decision (which in reality, he was making a negative decision), to accept Christ as Savior. He told me it was too easy to be true. There just had to be more to it. Christ made salvation easy so that anyone and everyone could find New Life in Christ and become free from condemnation (Judgment).

To bring the Crusade to a climax, it was decided to have the final meeting elsewhere, because of the anticipated crowd. On Sunday, September 27, 1964, a crowd gathered in front of the State Capital Building on what is known as the Boston Common. This is a park type place, atop the underground parking for the city. By the time of the service, there were faces as far as the eye could see. It was estimated that this concluding service had over 75,000 people gathered. To say one was inspired is to say it lightly.

This was to be the end of the Boston Crusade, but at this gathering it was announced that Billy Graham would be returning to Boston the following week from October 5-11. The need for the Gospel was too great to be ignored. Other scheduled Crusades in Seattle and Vancover, B.C. had to be re-scheduled to meet the Boston's concerns.

In addition to this, because the need was felt by the committees, 2 3-day Crusades were held in Bangor and Portland, Maine; Burlington and Montpelier, VT; Manchester and Concord, N.H.;

Providence, R.I.; and Worchester, MA during the months of October and November, 1964.

What have I learned by this experience?

The first thing is that there is JOY in serving Jesus Christ. Too many people who call themselves Christians are content with being spectators and taking in all the blessings that come their way. Little do they know that participation in the Lord's Work has far more blessings then we can possibly receive. The prophet Malachi says it this way: *"Bring all the tithes (of time, treasures and talents) into the storehouse , that there may be food in My house, and prove Me now in this, says the Lord of Hosts, 'If I will not open for you the windows of heaven and pour out for you such blessing that there will not be room enough to receive it."* *(Malachi 3:10)*

JOY can only be found in sharing the "Good News" of Christ and His Plan of Salvation. A blessing can only become fully appreciated as we share it with a member of the family, a friend, a neighbor or someone we meet for the first time.

Worry is the darkroom where negatives are developed

The Still
Small
Voice

Chapter Eleven

Jesus said, "Behold I stand at the door and knock. If anyone hears My voice and opens the door, I will come in to him and dine with him, and he with me."

"He who has an ear, let he hear what the Spirit says..."

Revelation 3:20, 22

LIFE is composed of both negative and positive experiences. The key to making one's life fulfilling and meaningful is to be able to distinguish between the two and let go of the negatives in our lives as soon as possible and keep firm hold of the positives, as long as you can. How we end up living our lives is determine by that which we hold onto and what we are willing to let go, and build there upon.

Much of my childhood remains a mystery to me. It could very well be because there are some negatives I have chosen not to remember. They could possibly answer some questions as to my being who I am, but I am content where my life has brought me thus far. I am happy with letting sleeping dogs lie. As one song writer would say, "Let bygones, be bygones, forever."

Serving as a pastor of smaller churches, as I have over my ministry, I have been invited to attend the "School of Evangelism" and/or "School of Missions", sponsored by the Billy Graham Evangelistic Association (B.G.E.A.). I took advantage of two of these events, with the assistance of scholarships provided by B.G.E.A., for which I am deeply appreciative. These scholarships are made available to pastors who's wages fall below what is considered average.

The first of these schools I attended was held on the Campus of Wheaton College in Wheaton, Illinois, at the Billy Graham Center located on the campus. My wife and son (not yet a teenage) were able to attend with me. We were invited to stay with a former pastor of mine, Dr. Morris A. Inch, and his wife Joan, when we lived in Massachusetts, during my high school and college years. He was then a Dean at Wheaton College and Joan worked as secretary in their church.

The school was held from Monday afternoon through Friday Morning. This was scheduled so the pastors who attended didn't have to find replacements in their respective churches on Sundays. The B.G.E.A. also assisted in paying milage, to help with the traveling expenses. There is much more to the Billy Graham Crusades than the services held in the Stadiums. In addition to these schools I have just mentioned, they give Bible Studies to all enquirers, provide good spiritual reading materials, produce excellent Christian Films, broadcast some of the Crusades on T.V., publish a magazine called "Decision", radio devotional programs called The Hour of Decision, mission endeavors and many other projects throughout the world.

In the Billy Graham Center there are all kinds of Evangelistic Memorabilia, going way back to the early Evangelistic Campaigns of past great Evangelists. There is also a sound-proof booth you can enter and record on tape a personal testimony or talk, that lasts three minutes. With your permission this could be used on the Billy Graham radio show, "The Hour of Decision".

The outstanding feature that will remain in my memory and that of my family, is the Scriptural Walk. Along the walls are engraved scriptural verses. There is a doorway in the shape of a "Cross".that you enter, representing the suffering that Christ had to go through on our behalf. As you go through the doorway, you enter a long winding corridor that is carpeted in black top, sides and bottom), representing the death that ALL sinners must pay for their sin, but Christ paid that price for us. At the end of this corridor there appears a bright light, with majestic music being sung by an angelic choir. As you come to this new entrance, you step as it were into mid-air. (A bit scary to say the least), with blue sky and clouds above you, under you, beside you, and all around you. This represents the Resurrection of Christ and all Believers, who have received Christ as Savior.

Words are inadequate to describe one's feelings and emotions at this moment. You just have to be there to feel the presence of the Holy Spirit, and the Joy of being part of the Family of God. If you are ever anywhere near Wheaton College, I would encourage you to take time to discover this feeling. You will not be disappointed.

The School of Evangelism, sponsored by the B.G.E.A. was held in Boston, Massachusetts in conjunction with another of the Crusades held in Boston. This particular crusade was held in the former Brave's Field Stadium, an open-air baseball field, seating thousands of people. I had attended this school by myself, (My wife and son remained in Michigan). We were housed in one of the hotels within the city. As was the other crusades, it began on Monday afternoon and ended on Friday morning.

We attended the various classes provided and listened to outstanding speakers during the day. Reserve seats were set aside in the evening, so those attending the school could attend the crusade. If my memory serves me well, it was not the greatest weather that week. It was decided at one of the meetings that an alter-call would be given but have the enquirers stay in their seats, because the field was too wet to walk upon. It didn't matter to the enquirers, seeing they came and stood in front of the platform, puddles and all.

As I entered the stadium the first meeting, I encountered a vast number of faces, as I looked around. It was like a sea of different faces looking at me. All of a sudden, I heard what sounded like a small voice, that stood out among the various conversations. I heard, "Harvey! Harvey! Harvey!" I stopped and looked around to where the voice seemed to come from. With so many people there, it was impossible to pick out one individual. I proceeded to my seat and again I heard that same voice, "Harvey! Harvey! Harvey!" This time it sounded a bit louder but I could not determine it's location. The third time I heard the same voice, (Much like what Samuel heard in the Old Testament - I Samuel 3:1-11). I said somewhat quietly, "Here I am, Lord, what do you want?" No reply came. I then sat down and enjoyed the crusade that evening. It wasn't until I returned to my room at the hotel and called my sister-in-law, Carol, that I found out that the voice I heard belonged to her. She and her husband John, had attended the crusade that evening.

It turned out to be a week of many blessings because of the school and the crusade. You may have watched one of the crusades on television, but it does not compare to being there in person. You have to be there to feel the presence of the Holy Spirit working through one of His servants. The only negative part of the week was that my wife, Norma and son, Mark were back in Michigan and I missed them greatly. It was good to get back home to share with them the events of the week and others in the church. To be blessed is great, but these blessings are not ours to keep to ourselves. Only when they are shared and given away can they become greater blessings, as they bless others. Blessings are like "Love". It is good to be loved, but when you give that love away, there is always room to receive more. There is no shortage, when it come to God's Love or His Blessings. *"Bring all the tithes - the whole tenth of your income - into the storehouse that there may be food in My house, and prove Me now by it, says the Lord of host, if I will not open the windows of Heaven for you and pour you out a blessing, that there shall not be room enough to receive it." (Malachi 3:10 - Amplified)*

What have I learned by this experience?

There is no end to our growing, by learning experiences. As long as we are alive, there is something new to learn, that will help in our growth, both physically and spiritually. Paul gave to young Timothy some great advice. *"Study to show thyself approved unto God, a worker who does not need to be ashamed, rightly dividing the word of truth." (II Timothy 3:15)*

It doesn't matter how many times you read a portion of scripture, you will always find something you hadn't seen before. The more you feed your soul with the Word of God, the stronger you become spiritually, and better able to fight off the forces of evil when they come to attack.

Another thing I have learned is that there is always someone out there who knows a bit more than I, and I can gain, not just knowledge, but wisdom from those who have experienced more. I don't believe there is anything original in my life. All I know and have has come by way of other people, whom I have met and had fellowship with over the years.

A lot of kneeling
Will keep you in good standing

Across the Waves

Waves

Chapter Twelve

Jesus said, "GO into all the world and preach the Gospel to every creature.

He who believes and is baptized will be saved; but he who does not believe will be condemned."

Mark 16:15,16

It all happened one Sunday Evening when a friend of mine told me of a radio program he had heard on his way to church. He told me it was about the life story of Harvey Thomas. This immediately captured my attention. I had heard of the program before this and listened on different occasions as I traveled throughout the city. It contained dramatizations of people or events of interest. The program is called "Unshackled" , sponsored by the Pacific Garden Mission in Chicago, Illinois. I was told this program was heard almost anywhere.

Having gained my interest, I decided to call the mission to seek a copy of the program, so I could listen to it. I told them what program I wanted to hear, even though I knew it was not about me, but another Harvey Thomas. I ended the conversation by telling them my name and address. I'm not sure what they were thinking at this moment. They did send the cassette which I listened to with great interest.

I had heard before, there was another Harvey Thomas somewhere (I would've thought one Harvey Thomas would be enough for the world to handle). I read about him years ago in one of Billy Graham's magazine entitle "Decision" . Mr. Thomas was then a fore-runner for the Billy Graham Evangelistic Crusades. He went a year before the scheduled Crusade to prepare the way; forming various committees for prayer, fund-raising, training of counselors and securing a location for the Crusade and getting things in order before the Crusade Team arrived.

It was quite interesting to hear about this second Harvey Thomas, even though we have never met, talked nor corresponded with each other. It sort of helped me realize that I am not alone in the work of serving the Lord Jesus Christ. It was like God created two of us to work in different parts of the world.

I didn't think much more about this after that. It was in November, 2005 when I received a letter from the Pacific Garden Mission containing a form to fill out. I was truly amazed to think that I had made such an impression on them months before. I thought to myself, "Who am I that I should be considered and honored in such a way as to have my life put on radio?" I am just an ordinary man attempting to share the Love of God and spread the Gospel of Christ in my small portion of the world, where I lived.

They wanted to know about who I was and my ministries with the churches I served and the Jails/prisons Ministry . I filled out the form and mailed it back to them along with a copy of my first published book, "The Key to Freedom from Captivity". This book contains more information about myself in its first chapter. Upon receiving this they proceeded to send out questionnaires to the references I had submitted.

In February, 2006, the coordinator of "Unshackled" called me at my home and we talked for about an hour and a half. She wanted more information of my early life and especially the details of my accepting Jesus Christ as my Savior. She informed me that the script for the program was being written by the writers as we spoke and she needed this info to complete it. As soon as it was finished she would send it my way. This call came on Saturday, Feb. 11th. On Monday, Feb. 13th I had the script in my hands ready for corrections and approval. . She asked that I call her the following day with any corrections so it wouldn't be delayed.

I was informed that the program number is #2893 (The number for the other Harvey Thomas is #2839). It was to be aired during the week of May 28th - June 3rd, 2006. During this week the program would have been heard some 6,500 times, somewhere in the world. It would be heard in 147 countries, covering all six continents and would be in eight languages: English, Spanish Arabic, Russian, Romanian, Polish, Korean and Japanese. WOW! (Who would have thought such a thing would happen to someone like myself?)

I still find it hard to believe I am that important. Then again all who serve God are not only important but also Special. It's kind of difficult to be humble when something like this happens. I know it is not because of what I have accomplished, but rather what God has been able to do through someone like myself and in spite of myself.

As of this writing, even though it has already been produced, I anxiously awaited to hear it, to see what the response would be (Especially hearing a Boston Accent in one of the foreign languages.). I gave it over to God, as I had my book, to use as He desires. After all it's not what I have done that matters (It's not about me), but what He has done through me (It's all about HIM). Without His help, guidance, provisions and power, I could have done so little to make a difference in this world. All that I do is for His Glory not mine. "To God be the Glory , great things He has done."

What have I learned by this experience?

A number of years ago when I was considered a young person, I attended the Christian Endeavor Society in my church. One of the things I enjoyed, as part of the program, was the learning and singing of Christian Choruses. Many of these have stayed with me over the years and I catch myself singing them from time to time. As I was writing of this experience, I was reminded of one of these choruses. The words of this chorus are quite fitting for this experience:

> "It's a good thing to be a Christian, it's the best thing I know.
> It's a good thing to be a Christian, no matter where you go.
> It will bring you joy and gladness, it will drive away your tears.
> It's a good, good thing to be a Christian, so BROADCAST the news."

(The authors/writers of this chorus is unknown, but I appreciate them in producing and publishing this years ago.)

One of the lessons I have taken from this experience is that we have an awesome God in control. We look at ourselves and wonder just who we are and why we are here. Many people look at themselves as nothing more than a biological product of their parents. Some even believe that they are nothing but an accident of their parents' relationship. The reality is that we are all creations of an almighty God.. God does not do anything by accident. All that He creates is for a purpose and has a design in His masterpiece, we call earth. We all have Special gifts and abilities that make us unique. If we are willing to use what He has given us for His Glory, He takes what we are able to do and expands it to reach out to the every person we met, to show His Love for them. He constantly amazes me what He is able to do with my life, as this experience well illustrates.

Growing Old is Mandatory Growing Up is Optional

Living with Mother Nature

Chapter Thirteen

*"You are a chosen generation, a royal priesthood,
a holy nation. His own special people, that you may
proclaim the praises of Him, who called you out of
darkness into His marvelous Light:"*

I Peter 2;9

As a young person I don't ever remember attending a summer camp, mainly because coming from a family of eleven children, the money just wasn't there for such extra activities. I can't say that I missed out an anything because I had never had that experience. I was content with what I had and was thankful for it. I never considered us poor until someone said we were. I was just happy being who I was and where I was.

It wasn't until I was in my late teens that I had my first experience, not as a camper but as a counselor at a Y.M.C.A. camp in Sanbornville, N.H. We stayed in cabins with eight campers along with the counselor. The campers were in a large area together and the counselor had a small room by himself. I was there for the summer, not just a week. Being a green-horn as it was, I am sure I was taken advantage of many times by the campers. They had been there before, I had. They seemed to know their way around better than I knew.

I was to be in charge of the Arts and Crafts along with being a counselor. During this activity they made plaster of Paris figurines and painted them. We also made bracelets, wrist bands and lanyards using gimp, which is plastic lancing in various colors, making leather belts, name bracelets and lacing wallets together. Perhaps you have made something like these in your camping experience..

The staff was there for the summer, 24/7 with one day off to get away from the kids and the work. Believe me there were weeks when we needed to get away, even for a short while. I took advantage by making good use of any free time, I had on or off the camp grounds. One day I even walked 3 miles to town and back.

Being a new counselor, my campers decided to play a prank on me while I was on a day off. Nothing out of the ordinary as far as camp pranks go. They knew I would be gone until late at night, After they had been put to bed for the evening, that is when they decided to execute their plans.

----- They decided to unscrew all the light bulbs, so I couldn't see where I was going when I got back.
----- They carefully draped toilet paper all around the door to my room, every which-way
----- They placed round cloth-pins on the floor, all over. (I'm not sure where they got them.)
----- They picked up stones (all sizes) and placed them in my bed, under the covers.
----- They short-sheeted my bed. (Folding the inner sheet half way and tucked it in.)
----- The set my alarm clock to go off around 3:00 a.m. (You can see they probably had done this before to some poor soul.) It was carefully planned.

I didn't get back to the cabin that night until after midnight. Not desirous to wake the campers, I didn't attempt to turn on any lights.

I didn't just walk in as I normally would, I tip-toed in and missed stepping on any of the rounded cloth-pins. Feeling my way in the dark, I felt the toilet paper that covered the doorway. Upon sitting on the bed I was able to feel the lumps made by the stones and removed them right away. By this time I was sure that the bed had been short-sheeted, so I remade the bed so I would be able to get in without difficulty, as tired as I was, I immediately got in the bed and went to sleep until the next morning. What about the alarm clock you might be asking? The clock was one that had to be wound every day. I was so tired I had forget to wind the clock. The clock stopped just prior to the 3:00 a, m, alarm.

Nothing that was so carefully planned worked out. Needless to say the campers were not happy campers that morning. I made no mention of the past night's events and just went about my daily tasks. This didn't go well with the campers either. I had to get back at them some how. When the time was right and unexpected, you can be sure I did. I, nonetheless, had a very pleasant experience at camping that summer.

My next camping experience was when I went to camp with my brother, Willis (known by most as Will or Billl). He worked for the Boys and Girls Clubs of America. We went to camp this summer with different responsibilities. I was to be a counselor and director of the Arts and Crafts. Much like my past experience, except we had ceramics as part of the program. We had to pour the liquid clay into molds and wait for them to dry. They were then fired in the kilm, painted and fired once again. Being a veteran, experienced counselor, I had a very enjoyable summer with little difficulty.

This was the end of my camping experience until I had finished college and entered the Christian Ministry, as a Pastor. While ministering in Michigan, a fellow pastor was directing a week's camp at our denominational campsite. It was located in the Upper-lower Peninsula. (Michigan, if you are not aware, has two Peninsulas (the Upper and the Lower).

I was not to serve as a counselor, but be the Camp Pastor for the week. It didn't take long before it was discovered that one of the counselors snored so bad, he kept the campers up all night. He was moved into a cabin by himself so everyone could get a good night's sleep. I was asked to take over the cabin for the rest of the week. Just added responsibility. As Camp Pastor I was in charge of all the spiritual gatherings - morning devotions, late afternoon vespers and campfire talk. I also took part in the various group activities, such as capture the flag, water-gun battles (hunting for the counselors) and water Olympics.

It was customary to throw one of the campers and/or staff member into the lake after the evening meal. The persons who received the most mail that day was elected to get thrown in the lake. It just so happened that I was to celebrate my birthday during that week. All of my so-called friends and family members made sure I received many, many cards and letters. I really think the staff held up all my mail until my birthday. You guessed it - in the lake I went.

My greatest experience at this camp came when I was asked to give my testimony at the camp-fire one night. All of the boy and girl campers were present along with a number of the staff personal. We sang many of the familiar camp songs, singing loud enough so the Methodist Camp could hear us across the lake. It's always a good time when we get together to sing and laugh, not only at camp but anywhere where people of like values gather.

Near the close of the camp-fire when the ambers of the fire were glowing brightly, I gave my testimony as to how God played a part in my life, from youth through my ministry in the Church. I closed my talk with an invitation for anyone who desired a closer relationship with Christ. Soon a few of the campers stood up and came closer to the fire for a word of prayer. Others soon followed. Before I knew it, everyone of the campers and staff members had gathered around the fire, except for one boy who was a Muslim. I believe he wanted to come forward but didn't want to do anything that was contrary to his parent's beliefs. I had never seen the working of the Holy Spirit as I did that night. We closed our time together that evening with prayer for one another. The group broke up, using their flashlights to find their way back to their cabins for evening devotions. This truly was an experience that I will never forget as long as I live.

Two of my campers in the cabin were brothers. They were like a pair of gloves. Where you found one you found the other.. We kept in communication over the years. The phrase we kept using is "You Guyzzzzzz". Many letters have been written using this phrase. Unfortunately the younger of the two was killed in an automobile accident on Father's Day when he was just out of high school. I had his funeral, which was most difficult. His older brother did get himself in trouble with the law and was sent away for a few years. He is out now, trying to get his life back together. We do keep in touch from time to time.

There have been many happy memories in my camping experiences. Many of the campers I will never forget. I do have group pictures which I look at from time to time and smile as I relive these precious moments.

What have I learned by this experience?

When God created us He threw away the mold. There has never been and never will be another person like you or me, even if you are an identical twin or triplets. We have our very own finger prints and D.N.A. Being unique as we are, that makes us not only important but very SPECIAL in the sight of God. He has planned our lives from before our birth to our death on this earth. He, alone knows our weaknesses and strengths. He has planned our lives around what will make us happy. All we have to do is follow His lead. He said it to His disciples and He says it to us. "Follow Me".

The smallest good deed is better than the grandest intention.

Physically

     challenged

Mentally

     alert

Morally

     straight

Chapter Fourteen

"For you are a holy people to the LORD your God; the LORD your God has chosen you to be a people for Himself, a special treasure above all the peoples on the face of the earth."

Deuteronomy 7:6

"Today the LORD has proclaimed you to be His special people, just as He has promised you, that you should keep all His commandments."

Deuteronomy 2 7:18

W HEN our son started school we became aware that his development was somewhat slower than that of most of the other children. We decided at that time to have him tested by the school authorities to see what the problem was. They found it difficult to classify him, so they put him under the L.D. Classification (Learning Disability) This simply meant that he has his own way of learning, apart from the standard educational methods. As a result he was placed in Special Education classes for his Academic Education.

As he got older we were told he was eligible to participate in the Special Olympic Program for the physically and educationally challenged students. We decided to allow him to participate if he so desired. We felt he needed this type of interaction with people with special needs to give him a sense of independence, especially from his parents..He participated mainly in basketball, soccer, and bowling. As a result, he was awarded many medals (gold, silver and bronze along with 4th place ribbons) for his effort.

This is how I became connected with the Special Olympics over these past years. I am presently a certified bowling coach for the Special Olympics. One cannot find a better group of young people to work with than those who are truly challenged (Handicapped as most people would call them.) The reality of it all is that we are all handicapped in one way or another, if we would be honest with ourselves.

My wife and I would often go to the various tournaments, local and state, to show our support for him and his friends. I would have to return home on Saturdays as I had to preach on Sunday Mornings. It was at these events that he and the others were awarded the medals and ribbons recognizing their participation and efforts. It really didn't matter which they received. They cheered and supported each other's efforts and achievements. A great time was had by all, both the Olympians , coaches and parents.

I remember at one of the state soccer tournaments held near Detroit, MI, I cheered and cheered for our home team. I lost my voice before the evening ended. It was a Saturday and I had to preach the next morning in church. Not kowing what would happen the night before I entitled the sermon, "The Silence of God" . Quite fitting wouldn't you say?   It was too late to try to get a fill-in speaker. I didn't know what I was going to do. I left it in God's hand to take care of it. I was able to preach, but with someone else's voice that Sunday.

As my son got older, we decided we would let him go with the group without our presence. He needed to learn some independence. He needed the break and so did his parents. It was difficult the first few times but he acclimated. Each time away it got easier and easer.

Throughout his Special Education, he participated in the after school activities (mainly bowling).About 40 students took part, each having their own special challenge in life. Some were like my son, (not badly disabled), others .had more physical disabilities and some were in wheelchairs. The physical appearances had no baring on their fun together. They just enjoyed being together and having fun.

It wasn't long before the students from Hillsdale College began to be part of these activities. They formed what is known as the "Best Buddies" group. They met with the kids each week and offered assistance, instruction and encouragement. Some weeks we had as many college students as we did these special needs young people. Eventually the college began to plan some special activities for the kids, at the college. They were invited to attend sports games, picnics, movies, and dances. They began an Annual Day of Champions, where outstanding speakers came. They played games 'till they hearts were content. Some of the college students received credits for their education, but many just came to help

I personally take great pleasure working with people who just enjoy being around people, regardless who they are or how they look. Getting to know the inside person is far more important and seeing the outside person only. If only we could capture the view these special needs young people have, and adopt it as our own, we would have a far better world to live in.

Even our International Olympians can learn what true sportsmanship is all about by observing the way these Special Olympians conduct themselves, win or lose the Gold. It's not about what award we gain but how we play the game or run the race that really matters. It needs to be more than receiving medals or prestige as one participates in the games. All Olympians need to adopt the oath of the Special Olympics:

> "Let me win -
> If I cannot win
> Let me be brave
> In the attempt."

What have I learned by this experience?

My hat goes off to all the Special Olympians, those who are volunteer coaches, the college students who support and encourage, the parents who allow their child(ren) to participate and all who give contributions to make Special Olympics possible . Let's not place these "Special People" in the shadows where they cannot be seen and enjoyed by all. Observing them closely, we will learn the lessons all people need to know and practice what we profess. The world can only become a better place if we do.

One who lacks the courage to start, has already finished.

Stormy
Weather

Chapter Fifteen

"A great windstorm arose, and the waves beat into the boat, so that it was already filling. He (Christ) was in the stern, asleep on a pillow. And they awake Him and said to Him, 'Teacher, do You not care that we are perishing?' He arose and rebuked the wind, and said to the sea, "Peace, be still!" and the wind ceased and there was a great calm. He said to them, 'Why are you so fearful? How it that you have no faith?' They feared exceedingly and said one to another, "Who can this be, that even the wind and the sea obey Him?"'

Mark 4:37-41
(N.K.J.)

S TORMY weather is part of what Mother Nature provides. There just doesn't seem to be any way around the storms. Whenever we think of storms, we think only of the negative effects they cause.

Every year we fearfully anticipate the hurricanes that usually appear between the months of June through November. Storms come in many forms; hurricanes, tornadoes, cyclones, title waves, snow, sleet, sand and wind storms to mention only a few. Which of these will effect us depends largely upon our location on earth.

There are many other types of storms that come our way during our lifetime; financial, marital, health, death, separation, divorce and unemployment, to name just a few. I believe there are times when it seems like we're hit with almost all of them at the same time. They make us feel and question as to why should we go on?

My first stormy experience that I can remember happened when I was about seven (7) years of age. I remember little of my childhood, but this stands out. My brother and I were running up and down our street, pouncing in all the water puddles we could find. In those days the young people had to find things to entertain themselves. We didn't have the funds to buy expensive toys, but at least we got the exercise out bodies needed. It was long before television (as we know it today) video games, computers, that kids have today. We didn't have the electronic technology that kids have to occupy their time. (far too often in my estimation.)

I didn't know then, as I do now, the fierceness of what we call hurricanes. This happened in 1939, I believe. We didn't know we were suppose to be afraid, so we just enjoyed the rain while we could. I learned to fear them, thereafter. Today I would stay inside when one is predicted. I've seen and heard the change and damage it can cause, as I am sure you have as well.

Since my early childhood many storms have found their way into my life. Death has been a heavy burden between the years of 1968 - 1970 . During this time I lost my one and only grandmother (the other three grand parents died before I was born), two uncles on my mother's side, my father and mother, a younger brother and younger sister, a nephew, a daughter (still born) and a father-in-law. Too many deaths to deal with in such a short period of time. These were certainly stormy days for me and my family. Just recently I have lost my older brother and older sister, within a week of each other. I have also lost recently a dear collogue in ministry who is responsible for my ordination, the late Rev. Thom Black.

When I proposed marriage to the one I fell in love with, I didn't know how much of a stormy marriage that could become. We got married in February, 1969 on a Saturday afternoon. The reception was to be at the church we got married in. The sun was shining, a beautiful day to get married.

After the reception we got ready to leave for our honeymoon at Cypress Gardens in Florida. We left about 4:00 p.m. and headed south. When we stopped in New Jersey, we heard that a major snow storm had hit all of New England. All who traveled any distance for the wedding got stranded.

It rained very hard as we continued our journey south to South Carolina. We planned to stay with my bother there overnight. When we left there an ice storm hit the area. We traveled on to Tampa, Florida. While there, we visited the Cypress Gardens and Bush Gardens. We went across the state to the east coast to visit my wife's aunt. We really had a great time while we were there. We spent a week in Florida all together.

Upon leaving, heading back home, Florida received another one of their storms which made difficult traveling. We stopped again in South Carolina overnight. They again experienced stormy weather. When we finally arrived back in Massachusetts, a second major snow storm hit the area. My wife and I resolved not to get married again. We had upset the weather pattern wherever we went.

It was during the year of 1978 that most of the east coast, especially New England, got hit with a major snow storm during that weekend. It snowed so rapidly that the plows were not able to keep up with the snow and had to stop. All the major highway and interstates were closed with many travelers stranded, not even able to leave their vehicles. They had to stay put until someone was able to rescue them..

It was so bad that the governor declared a state of emergency, and closed all roads to any and all vehicles for a week. The City of

Somerville, where I lived, went a step further and declared a second week of closure because there was no way the streets could be cleared. There was no sense in trying to leave the house. There was no where we could go. Snowmobiles were put in use to help those who needed medical assistance or medicines.

During those two weeks my family got the flu. We stayed put and tried not to move around too much in the house. Our neighbor (an elderly man in his 80's) kept calling us to see if all was going well, He saw the lights on in our house but didn't see them go off or on. I don't know what he could have done for us, but it sure was comforting to know that someone cared. I was so sick that I didn't bother to shave for two weeks. I not only didn't feel good, I didn't look good either. After all was said or done, I did get around to shaving but kept the mustache for a year or longer. All the stores were completely emptied, because there was no way to replenish their supplies. Fortunately we had enough food in to keep us going.

My family and I also experienced some financial storms as we ministered together over the years. At one of my pastorates, one of the families thought I wasn't fulfilling my contract with the church. (I didn't know I was under any sort of contract.) I was under the belief that I was serving God not man. He was the One I had to answer to, not the church. The church was there to supply the needs for the one God sent their way to minister.

About my third year into this pastorate, the church (under the influence of this discruntaled family) decided to drop my benefits (My medical and retirement insurance). God didn't chose to move me that year, so the church cut my salary in half due to the lack of funds, so arranged by this disgruntled family. God and I had a discussion about this matter. He again decided to leave me where I was. The fifth year there, the church had no choice but to cut my salary completely, but they allowed me to live in the parsonage, if I continued to preach on Sundays. This family was too influential. No church should be controlled by any one family. God and I got together once again about this matter. I was kept on for an additional year. All I could do was to stay where God had put me, until He decided to move me elsewhere.

That final year God proved His faithfulness to those who remain faithful to Him. God's work, done God's way will never lack God's supply. You just have to keep the faith and trust God to do what He says He will do.

There have been many other storms in my life and in the lives of my family that we were able to weather. Not because we are such great people, but because of our God promised never to leave us nor forsake us. We constantly feel His presence with us as we strive to do His will.

Usually after the rain clouds come and go, we discover something beautiful happens. If you look closely you might discover a beautiful rainbow appears in the sky.

The rainbow first appeared in scripture after God decided to destroy all living things, via the flood in Noah's day (Genesis 7-9). Only Noah , his wife, their three sons and their wives were saved. It rained for forty days and forty nights, continuously. After living for more than a year in the ark, among two of every kind of animal on earth, God displayed a beautiful rainbow. This was to be a sign of God's Promise, never would He (God) destroy the world again with a flood.

If you look closely in the sky after a rain storm, you will discover that it is made up of seven colors. A. C. Dixon in his book, "The Bright Side of Life" (pages 40-42) says the seven colors of the rainbow represent the seven promises of God's dealing with the matter of the sin question (each color is more brilliant then the one before):

1. The Promise of FORGIVENESS - I John 1:9

    "If we confess our sins, He is faithful and just to <u>forgive us</u> our sins and to cleanse us from all unrighteousness."

2. The Promise of CLEANSING - I John 1:7

"If we walk in the light as He is in the light, we have fellowship with one another, and the blood of Jesus Christ His Son cleanses us from all sin. "

3.   The Promise of COVERING OCEAN-DEEP - Micah 7:19

"He will again have compassion on us, and will subdue our iniquities. You will cast all our sins into the depths of the sea."

4.   The Promise of INFINITELY REMOVED - Psalm 103:12

"As far as the east is from the west, so far has He removed our transgressions from us."

5.   The Promise of being BLOTTED OUT - Isaiah 41:22

I have blotted out, like a thick cloud, your transgressions, and like a cloud, your sins return to Me, for I have redeemed you."

6.   The Promise of NOT MENTIONING IT TO US-Ezekiel 33:16

"None of his sins which he has committed shall be remembered (mentioned) against him; he has done what is lawful and right; he shall surely live."

7.   The Promise of FORGETTING - Hebrews 8:12

"I will be merciful to their unrighteousness and their sins and their lawless deeds. I will remember no more."

What have I learned by this experience?

Someone once said that there are Silver Linings in the clouds. What is meant by this is that there is some good that can be found in our storms of life, if we are willing to stop and recall all that took place. The Apostle Paul says it best as he wrote to the church in Rome: *"We know that all things work together for good to those who love God, to those who are called according to His purpose."* *(Romans 8:28).*

Anna Campbell and B.D. Ackley wrote a hymn that is a constant reminder of the Promises of the rainbow:

There's a Rainbow shining somewhere!
:
When the cares of life assail me,
Then I search the skies above;
For the God who will not fail me
Sends an emblem of His love.
When the darkness falls around me,
When the clouds above my door
Come to say that trouble's found me,
Then I watch the skies once more.

God will come to heal my sorrow,
God will come to bring me peace,
With a rainbow on the morrow,
When the storms of life shall cease.

Chorus:
There's a rainbow shining somewhere,
There's a light across the skies;
There's a rainbow shining somewhere,
Like a gleam from Paradise;
Though today the clouds are drifting
Far across the stormy sea,
There's a rainbow shining somewhere,
That will some day shine for me.

If you want your dreams to come true, Don't oversleep.

Pennies From Heaven

Chapter Sixteen

"Do not lay up for yourselves treasures on earth, where moth and rust destroys and where thieves break in and steal; but lay up for yourselves treasures in heaven, where neither moth nor rust destroys and where thieves do not break in and steal. For where your treasure is, there your heart will be also. "

Matthew 6:19-21

Money has from the beginning of time played an important role in lives of all human beings. Before the birth of Christ the people had taxes to be paid. This is the reason Mary and Joseph had to go to Bethlehem to be counted and to be taxed by those in authority. Christ, as an adult used a coin, obtained from a fish (Matthew 17:27), as an object lesson for the Pharisee (Matthew 22:15-22; Mark 1212:13-17; Luke 20:20-26). He said to them *"Show Me the tax money...Whose image and inscription is this?... Render therefore to Caesar the things that are Caesar's and to God the things that are God's. "* No one likes to pay taxes, but how else can the governments operate, unless they have the funds to do so?

Unfortunately some governments go to an excess when taxing its citizens. On the other hand many citizens rob God by not giving Him what is rightly His, through His Church, the monies needed to operate effectively in their respective communities.

How many times in your travels have you spotted a penny on the ground? People have been known to throw away pennies rather than carrying them because of their weight and they consider them of little value. I have picked up many a penny over the years. You are aware that they do add up to great value in time. 100 pennies make a dollar.

"In Jessup, MD. A truck carrying 4.3 million pennies turned over at an entrance to a highway...Traffic was tied up for several hours...One penny alone...would not have held up anything but when 4.3 million pennies were brought together, they stopped traffic." (Encyclopedia of 7700 illustrations, #3534).

I read recently about a man who always stooped down to pick up a penny. When asked "Why?" he said that every time he picked one up, he took the time to examine it. Each time he saw stamped on it the words, "In God We Trust". This was a constant reminder to him that God is still on His throne and can be trusted.

Not too long ago I reached into my pocket and took out the change I had there. I picked out a few pennies to use as an illustration to some young people. In the process I discovered that one of the pennies was quite different from all the others. I examined it more closely and saw that it had part of the back side stamped on the front side. I believe this is called being doubled stamped. It is a 1983 copper penny. The back side of it had also been doubled stamped. The word "AMERICA" on the front was stamped backwards. This truly is different in every respect from any penny I had seen before. Needless to say, it got immediately separated from all the other coins and was kept secure. I can't imagine how this penny floated around since 1983, anywhere and everywhere, and not be noticed is beyond my understanding. I am thankful it finally reached me. I'm not sure how I obtained it, perhaps in change somewhere along the line. It is no longer in circulation.

I have been offered varied amount of money for my penny, but I am sure it is worth more than it's face value. I guess I'll keep it to see what it will bring before I try to sell it. I am not a coin collector, even though I have a few silver coins in my possession. Money is worthless unless you spend it for something. I suppose I could hold onto this penny and never really go broke. " Too many people spend money they haven't earned, to buy things they don't really want, to impress people they don't like." (#3543 I.E.)

There are some people who believe that money is the root of all evil. Nowhere in scripture can anyone find this saying. What we will find is: *"For the LOVE of money is a root of all kinds of evil, for which some have strayed from the faith, in their greediness, and pierced themselves through with many sorrows." (I Timothy 6:10 N.K.J.)*

What have I learned from this experience?

God uses the common, ordinary, everyday things to accomplish His Divine Plans in our lives. We just have to be alert, open our eyes and explore the many opportunities we so often overlook in our busy, get-things-done, way of living. Try to relax and look around and see what God provides to bring happiness .and blessings into our lives. We miss so many when we get too self-absorbed and self-centered.

The 10 Commandments are not Multiple Choice

The Lazarus Tree

Chapter Seventeen

Jesus said, "I am the resurrection and the life, He who believes in Me , though he may die, he shall live. And whoever lives and believes in Me shall never die. Do you believe this?"

John 11:25,26
N.K.J.

TREES have always played an important part in human life from the beginning of time. Trees are first mentioned in the Garden of Eden when God created all that ever existed: *"And the earth brought forth grass, the herb that yields seed according to its kind and the tree that yields fruit, whose seed is in itself to its kind, and God saw that it was good. So the evening and the morning were the third day." (Genesis 1:12,13 - N.K.J.)* Martin R. De Haan II in his pamphlet entitle "Celebrating the Wonder of a Tree" states: "a world without trees would be a vastly different place. Neighborhoods without trees, fields without woods, and continents without forests would mean the end of life as we know it."

According to this same pamphlet "Celebrating Trees", a list is given showing the importance of trees to all of life:

----- Provides oxygen
----- Moderates temperature
----- Collect and absorbs dust and other atmospheric pollutants.
----- Protects the earth from rapid climate change.
----- Produce and protect healthy soil.
----- Provides food.
----- Provides shelter and/or cover for many animals and birds.
----- Provides protection from thousands of species of sun-sensitive plants.
----- Provides healing products.
----- Provides wood.
----- Provides fuel
----- Provides sensory stimulation and the experience of beauty
----- Provides living fences that hold back drifting sand and snow.
----- Reduces light intensity from the sun.
----- Provides privacy
----- Protects watersheds for communities.
----- Produces a sense of rootedness and community.

It was the tree in the center of the Garden of Eden that Satan used to tempt Adam and Eve, that resulted in the Fall of Mankind from Fellowship with God, the Creator (Genesis 3). It took another tree to restore the Fellowship that was broken. This tree is called "Calvary" where Jesus Christ died and paid the Price for the sin of mankind. (Matthew 27:45-56). Because of Calvary, man is given a "Second Chance" to make amends with God and be given not only physical life but Eternal, Everlasting Life. Jesus Christ said to His disciples: *"...I have come that they may have life, and that they may have it more abundantly." (John 10:10b)*

While pastoring a church in Michigan, I was given a sapling of a red maple tree. I decided to plant this tree next to the parsonage. I watered it and cared for it until it began to grow on its own. One day while I was cutting the grass, I was using a weed-wacker to trim around it. As I approached this small red maple tree, I came too close to the tree and ended up cutting the bark off, all around the tree. I was not immediately aware of what I had just done, namely killing the tree. Those around me made sure I became aware of this dreadful fact. After a period of time the inevitable came true - the tree surely did die.

I let it die completely before I decided to cut it down with great pain. There wasn't much else I could do. Shortly thereafter, I discovered something growing. It was the tree beginning to grow again from its roots. It's been a few years and the tree has grown to be quite tall today. That is why I call it my "Lazarus Tree". Once it had died and came back to life as did Lazarus, a friend of Christ's (John 11:38-44)

There is another tree I would like to have considered at this point. It is one that we are all a part. It is called the "Family Tree". We all have one, wether we like it or not. Every family is part of two Family Trees. One on the Mother's side and one on the Father's side. The Family Tree on my side, I know very little about. I only know of the branches of my immediate family. My wife's Family Tree is another story. On her mother's side we have a tree that is in three volumes. It is the Studebaker Family Tree. My wife's mother is Gertrude Mae (Studebaker) Newton. Her great grand parents were the maker of the automobile and the Conestoga wagons. These wagons were used when our country decided to move west in its growth as a nation. The family homestead is located in Tipp City, Ohio. It is here that the Family Reunions are held every five years. (A week-end affair.)

I believe that my Mother-in-law is one of the oldest members of the Studebaker Family. A few weeks ago the family gathered at her home, where she lives alone in a three bedroom ranch and does her own cooking and cleaning. She gave up her driver's license just a couple of years ago. We gathered there for the purpose of celebrating her 100th Birthday. She was born on April 29, 1906. She received Greetings from the White House in Washington D.C. from President George W. Bush and his wife Lora. She also received Greetings from the Governor's Office in Harrisburg, PA. The Studebaker Family Association wrote an article in their quarterly Newsletter (Spring,

2006 issue). She also received over 200 Birthday Cards from her family members and friends.

We all are part of a Family Tree. Some trees are stronger than others and able to withstand the storms of life, while others have not a strong root system. The more we become rooted to our Creator, the stronger we will become. The question to answer is: "Where are you and your family roots grounded?" Hopefully it will be found in Christ Jesus. Martin Luther wrote: "God writes the gospel, not in the Bible alone, but also our trees, and in the flowers and clouds and stars." (Celebrating the Wonder of a Tree) God reveals Himself through the lives of those who have turned control over to the leading of the Holy Spirit.

How's your Family Tree? Is it growing day by day, month by month and year by year? Does it blossom with many blessings that are overflowing? Does it and will it continue to produce fruit that will enrich the lives of all who come in contact with it?

Joyce Killmer (1886-1918) once wrote a poem, I learned many years ago. It goes like this:

> I think that I shall never see
> A poem lovely as a tree .
> A tree whose hungry mouth is prest
> Against the earth's sweet flowing breast;
> A tree that looks at God all day,
> And lifts her leafy arms to pray;
> A tree that may in summer wear
> A nest of robins in her hair;
> Upon whose bosom snow has lain;
> Who infinitely lives with rain,
> Poems are made by fools like me,
> But only God can make a tree.

What have I learned by this experience?

We live in a day when many things appear to be hopeless. We just can't seem to find a reason to go on. We tend to give up easily rather then put forth a little effort to see the possibilities that lie before us. Giving up on things should never be acceptable in this day and age. It's so much easier to throw up our hands and throw in the towel then to see what can really happen with a little effort. When we reach our limits, that is when God steps in and provides what is lacking.

Christ made it possible for Lazarus to come back to life with a purpose in mind. He allowed my dead tree to take on new life. He can also give life to our endeavors if we are willing to work with Him. There is New Life in Jesus Christ.

If God is your co-pilot change seat.

Reflections

Chapter Eighteen

Community Baptist Church

"When I was a child, I spoke as a child, I understood as a child, I thought as a child; but when I became a man, I put away childish things. For now we see in a mirror, dimly, but then face to face. Now I know in part, but then I shall know just as I also am known."

I Corinthians 13:11,12
N.K.J.

Eᴀʀʟɪᴇʀ in this book, I have written a section entitled, "Stormy Weather" (Chapter 15), dealing with our wedding and honeymoon experience. This is another chapter of one of these experiences.

Hardly a day goes by that we don't have an opportunity to literally look at ourselves. We do it every morning when we awaken from a night of sleep. We wash ourselves in a shower or sink and groom ourselves to start the day. Throughout the day we take a glimpse or two in a mirror to make sure our hair (those who have hair that is.) is in place or make- up is still there. In the evening we look again, to dress up for a social event or gathering with other people. We become so self-absorbed that we often forget to look around at the beauty that God has created for our pleasure. Someone once said that we need to stop once in a while to smell the roses. God has given us a beautiful planet in which to live. Mother Nature gives us a beautiful glimpse into the beauty of God Himself, through nature.

While my wife and I were on our honeymoon, we made it a point to spend a little time at Cypress Gardens in Florida. This was to be our focal point, to begin our lives together as husband and wife. We wanted our focus to be on God through the beauty He provided for our enjoyment.

In the Cypress Gardens there were many rolling hills, beautiful flowers, trees and a lake where water skiing events took place. We couldn't help but notice the beautiful young ladies dressed in colorful hoop dresses, scattered throughout the grounds.

We came across a stand in our walking around, where we could place our camera and take a picture of ourselves. (Often times travelers need someone else to take the picture). The scene before us was beautiful to gaze upon. We couldn't let this photogenic opportunity escape. It was a gorgeous day for taking pictures. The only thing wrong was that we were not able to walk the paths before us, smell the beautiful flowers of all sorts, and colors or touch the things Mother Nature provided. You see we were only looking at a reflection of the real things. Yes, we were standing in front of a rather large mirror. In order to appreciate all the blessing that God provided for our pleasure, we had to turn around to see reality and all that it provided for our enjoyment.

I am waiting patiently and looking forward to the day when I will be able to see things as God see them. We will also be able to see and understand people as God does. Until then we have to be satisfied with whatever it is that God makes available to us.

On the back cover of a book I am presently reading, entitles "How to Keep Your Life in Focus" by Garth W. Coone, we find the following words printed: "Are you ready for a new vision? There is an exciting world God wants you to discover. You will never experience it, however, without a clear focus..."

Don't you agree with me, it is about time to stop looking at reflections that are untouchable and turn around and face the beautiful reality of life that God has provided for our enjoyment and pleasure? Despite the many valleys we travel through, there are many wonderful, beautiful mountain-top experiences for us to take advantage of that encompass our daily walk.

What I have learned by this experience?

If you are like me, we would like to be able to see into the future, so we would make the right decisions and the right choices. Most of the time it is to our benefit that we are kept in the dark. The future will, I am sure, scare us.

If I had known beforehand the difficulties I would face in the ministry, I doubt if I would have traveled this road. I would no doubt choose an easier, more profitable and more comfortable path. We are called upon to walk by faith, believing in God. He leads us step by step and as we look back we are amazed as to what God has brought us through and how He has used us to and for His Glory.

As I was preaching one Sunday, in the congregation there was a lad under the age of a teenager. He was somewhat , what we would call, being mentally challenged. He was very attentive during my preaching each time he was present. As he was leaving one Sunday with his grand-parents, he shook my hand and said: "Thank You, Jesus." (You talk about a compliment). You see he didn't see me in the pulpit but rather the reflection of Jesus, speaking to him.

I recently read a book entitled "Loving God with All my Mind" written by Julie Ackerman Link. On pages 57-64, she tells and tries to explain Biblical faith in these words: "Biblical faith is not about taking risks; it's about taking on the identity of Jesus. It's not about having the audacity to do something rishky, it's about having the courage to do what is right. It's not about running in the dark, it's about walking in the light. It's not about believing what people say about God, it's believing what God says..

"Beyond Belief

"Whenever I hear the song 'God Is on Our Side,' I feel uneasy...

"Abraham Lincoly said, 'I do not boast that God is on my side, I humbly pray that I am on God's side.' (2 Chronicles 1:2).

"One of my favaoarite Peanuts comic strips features Charlie Brown saying to Snoopy, 'I hear you're writing a book on theology. I hope you have a good title.' Snoopy responds, 'I have the perfect title: *Has It Ever Occured to You That You Might Be Wrong?*

"The Greek word translated repent is *metonoia,* which means 'change your mind...'

"I once had a picture come to mind that helped me understand my faulty way of seeing spiritual things. I was thinking about the way the world is and the way Satan wants me to see it. I began imagining myself in a small, slow-moving picture. My back was to the camera, and in front of me were prison bars from one edge of the frame to the other - lift to right and top to bottom. My hands were gasping the bars, and my face was pressed between them. Beyond the bars was a beautiful field with lots of lush grass, a bubbling brook with a water fall, and beautiful flowering trees and plants that waved slightly in a soft warm breeze. But the bars kept me from enjoying any of it. I could only long for what I had no way of reaching. I would occasionally shake the bars or bang my head against them, but it was all a self-defeating attempt to get what I believed I could never have.

"As I watched, the presepctive started changing. Little by little the carera moved back, showing me more of the picture. At first I was startled to see the wide-open space behind me. But as the camera moved back further, I was even more startled to see that what was behind me was the beautiful place I was longing for. In front of me - beyond the bars - was only a mirror reflelclting it. As the camera moved back it also moved up, allowing me to see behind the mirror. And there was Satan, watching me through the one-way mrror, laughing because I had wasted so much time longing for his illusion. He knew all along that to get the real thing all I had to do was turn around."

In Ray C. Stepman's book, "Waiting for the Second Coming" (Pages 118, 119) we find these words: "Our glorification is based upon the fact that we have believed that Another did something for us. Another died in our place and God has honored that Other.

"Paul describes the glory of Jesus that will be seen 'in his holy people,' and the way these believers cause people to marvel at what God has done in human lives. It is not Jesus Himself and His glory that is described, but the saints reflecting the glory of Jesus. The whole universe will marvel.

"There is a glory, a joy, known only by the redeemed. That marvelous manifestation of the grace and glory of God will be evident in those who have been changed by His grace."

The best Vitamin for a Christian – "B-1"

NOT an Unclouded Day

Chapter Nineteen

Built - 1899

Present Structure

"While he was still speaking, behold, a bright cloud overshadowed them; and suddenly a voice came out of the cloud, saying, 'This is My beloved Son, in whom I am well pleased. Hear him'"

Matthew 17:5

W E call nature, "Mother Nature" for whatever reason there may be. If nature has to be called something other than what it actually is, maybe we should call it "Father Nature", seeing our heavenly Father (Almighty God) created all things (Genesis 1,2). Someone once said, "We should stop and smell the roses" (A good idea). I would suggest we need to stop and look at the clouds that hang above us. When we usually think of clouds, the first thing that comes to mind is that stormy weather awaits us. That seems to be the only thing they are good for.

I know I have written about clouds already, dealing with the storms in our lives. (Chapter 15 - Stormy Weather) This chapter I want to focus mainly on the clouds themselves. One of the constant activities of our God.

From the Encyclopedia of Illustration we learn "How to Interpret Clouds" "Meteorologists make suggestions such as these for interpreting the clouds: Quickly moving, lowering clouds at dinner time foreshadow poorer weather by breakfast. Billowing white clouds in summer indicate the likelihood of sudden showers. Dark clouds gathering on a western horizon betoken rain or snow. A cloud-filled summer sky at eventide betokens a hot night." (#7338)

My first real interest in clouds came as I made my first air-flight. It was rather a short venture as I flew from Boston to Worchester, MA, the sum total of 50 miles, hardly enough time for the plane to climb above the clouds. I was heading for the Grand Opening of a Super Market for whom I was working at the time. To my amazement, I was able to see God's wondrous work of creation as He sees it. I could hardly believe what we miss from the ground level.

Clouds generally are white and look like puff formations, good enough to lie upon and get a good night's rest. At other times they are gray and sometimes nearly black, which are threatening and frightful when accompanied by thunder and lighting. Our only wish is that they would move quickly and out of sight. They only promise bad times as long as they linger.

As I gazed upon the clouds from the plane's window, I was in awe as to their beauty from the other side, especially when the sun is brightly reflected upon them. I wondered at this time what those on earth saw as they looked up while I was looking down.. There's a good chance they were not looking at all.

My last flight, made last week, as I attended my brother's funeral, the clouds caught my attention once again. I was flying from Providence, R.I. to home in Michigan via Chicago, Il. From the very beginning in R.I., I observed from the window of the plane nothing but what appeared to be like a gigantic white sheet, draped across the sky, covering all view of land. I did not see any land mass until I neared my first destination, Chicago. I couldn't see the earth and they on earth couldn't see us. I have no idea what the weather was beneath us. They could very well have been experiencing a major rain storm while I was enjoying the sunshine. Every thing seemed to be at a stand still, having no visible evidence that we were moving at all. I was happy to see land at last, two hours later as we landed.

An interesting observation to this flight, apart from the clouds, is the time line. About eight o'clock in the morning, the pilot announced we were flying over Detroit, MI, which caught my attention, seeing this was my final destination. The strange thing about it is that I did not land in Detroit until 12 noon (four hours later). I had to fly to Chicago and with a layover, then fly back to Detroit. Isn't man's scheduling of time amazing? (4 hours of wasted time just sitting in a crowded plane and/or airport).

We often enjoy looking at the mountains around us, observing their beauty and adventurous experiences climbing them. (Chapter Nine - "Eleven - Eleven - Eleven"). This does not compare to the mountain-like formation of the other side of the clouds. You have to take the time to notice the real beauty of the clouds.

Man has tried to improve upon what God has created, to help with, what they consider to be a helping hand. (How can man improve on what God has so wondrously created? How is it we think we know better than God?).

Once again from the Encyclopedia of Illustration: "Seeding operations are widespread around the world, particularly in Russia, Australia, Israel, Switzerland, France, Italy and Canada. The Soviet Union "definitely spends more money on weather modification than any other country in the world," according to Ronald Lavoie, director of the Environmental Modification Office of the National Oceanic and Atmospheric Administration. In the U.S.A., costs of weather-modification programs to Government and private interest have been running about 20 million dollars a year. The Russians spend an estimated 100 million a year." (#7335).

I am reminded of the story of a scientist talking to God. He said man didn't need God's help anymore. They have achieved the knowledge so much so that they were able, not only to create man, but vegetation to sustain man. God asked if he was willing to prove it. The scientist said he would. He reached out and picked up a handful of dirt. (You see God made man from the dust of the ground. *"In the sweat of your face you shall eat bread till you return to the ground, for out of it you were taken; for dust you are, and to dust you shall return." (Genesis 2:19 NKJ).* God stopped the scientist immediately in his tracts and said, "That's My dirt, go create your own."

Consider the clouds today and stand in awe, as I have done and will continue to do. How can anyone say there is no God? They had better wake up to the facts before it is too late to appreciate all that God as given us to enjoy. The greatness of God is all around us, if only we will take the time to explore the wonders that God has created for our and His pleasure.

What have I learned by this experience?

God has given us many, many things in nature for us to enjoy, even though we often neglect to take notice. Nothing we are able to see, can compare to what beauty awaits all who become Children of God, in the life hereafter. We are able to be dazzled at the sunsets that come at the close of the day. In Heaven there will be no need for a sunset, for there will be no darkness there. There will only be one sunrise when we enter the Glory Land of our Savior. There will be no preaching of the Gospel of Salvation, because all who will be in heaven will have already been saved, through the Blood of Christ while on earth, there will be no sin to confess, for where God is, sin cannot exist. There will be no clouds or rain, only His glorious radiance. God will supply all that is needed in nature to provide for His children. We had better enjoy the things of nature while we still have the opportunity.

The hymn writer, Rev. J. K. Alwood says it best in His hymn,

"The Unclouded Day"

O they tell me of a home far beyond the skies,
O they tell me of a home far away;
O they tell me of a home where no storm-clouds rise,
O they tell me of an unclouded day
O the land of cloudless day,
O the land of an unclouded day;
O they tell me of a home where no storm-clouds rise,
O they tell me of an unclouded day.

If it matters to you
It matters to God

Precious
Jewels

Chapter Twenty

"What shall I render to the Lord for all His benefits toward me? - How can I repay Him, for all His bountiful blessings? I will lift up the cup of salvation and deliverance, and call on the name of the Lord. I will pay my vows to the Lord, yes, in the presence of all His people. Precious (important and no light matter) in the sight of the Lord is the death of His saints - His loving ones."

(Psalm 116:12-15 Amplified)

P LEASURE is one of the expectations that mankind has as a goal in life. They will do anything, pay any price (monetary or any other way) to find happiness. They want life to be happy, free from anxieties or unpleasant feelings. For the unsaved, life is uncertain and far too short of a duration. They are out to get all they can and enjoy it to the fullest. It doesn't matter who gets in their way.

True happiness is a "precious" result of one's true relationship with the Creator of all things, Almighty God. It was His desire from the beginning of creation, that those He created were to have personal Fellowship with Him. We are here for His pleasure, not our own (that's just an added blessing).

It was in the Garden of Eden, where God walked and talked with Adam and Eve, that is until they chose to be disobedient, by partaking of the fruit of the Tree of Knowledge of good and evil (Genesis 3:12), which resulted in death, both physical and spiritual. Evidently, they chose this over the Tree of Life in the same garden. Because of their failure to obey their Creator, they hid themselves from God, when He came to have Fellowship with them, as He usually did (Genesis chapter Three).

We can experience the "Preciousness of Happiness" every time we receive a blessing from God. God is always ready to bless His children. For a blessing to be fully enjoyed, one needs to share that blessing with some other person(s). The greatest happiness a person can experience is when we share God's Love with someone else, and see them accept God's Love personally, by receiving Jesus Christ as their Savior. This is why I have entitled this chapter "Precious Jewels"

It was in 1964, at one of the Billy Graham's Evangelistic Crusades, held in the former Boston Gardens in Boston, Massachusetts, that I experienced the joy one receives when I introduced a young man, whose name is like a Precious Jewel (Royal Diamond) to God's Plan of Salvation. He was one of many I counseled at the Crusade that week. I could tell right off that this young man was sincere. After showing him the "Steps of Commitment" (Chapter Ten - "Here I am Lord, Send Me" - pages 64,65), giving him the literature provided by the Crusade and having a word of prayer, we parted company. I didn't expect to be seeing him again, being that he traveled from Connecticut to Boston.

I received a letter from him shortly thereafter. He told me of the accident he had going home after the Crusade that evening. I believe only the car got the damage. He returned to the Crusade a few days later, he wrote. He said he was thankful he had received Christ as his Savior that night, seeing what could have happened on his way home. It could have resulted with him entering eternity, but now he was ready. We lost contact shortly thereafter. He went his way and I went mine.

A couple of years ago, I decided to see if there was a way to reach him and others I worked with at the Crusade. I called and located Royal's brother, who in turn gave me his present phone number. He was now married and living in Pennsylvania. I called and his wife (whom I did not know nor she me) answered. I told her my name. That was all that was needed. (Mind you, this has been over 40 years ago). You see whenever Royal gave a testimony in his church, he always made mentioned of my name, as the one who brought him to Christ. (That sure made my day, you better believe.) She was happy to hear from me. Royal was not at home. She told me when he would be there, so I could call back. She wasn't going to mention that I had called earlier, so that it would be a surprise for Him. I called back and he sure was. The unconnected finally got reconnected. This truly was a "Precious" moment for each of our lives. It sure was great to have fellowship once again, even if it was only on the phone.

Royal was only one of twenty-four people that I counseled at the Crusade. I tried to contact some of the others with little or no success. All I can do at present is to turn them over to the Holy Spirit and let Him do the follow-up that I couldn't. God doesn't expect us to do all things. He just wants us to do what we can and then He takes over to complete the task.

Not all things work out the way we would like. I remember talking with another young man who was attending the Massachusetts Institute of Technology (M.I.T.). I used the same approach with him after he came forward at the Crusade, the same scripture verses and literature, as I did with all I counseled. At the end of our conversation, he said he was not able to accept what I was offering. His reasoning was that he could not accept Christ as Savior. It simply was "too easy" for it to be true. This was one of those times when knowledge got in the way of logic. We parted company at this point. He went back into the world without Christ in his heart. My prayer is that he, somewhere along the way, he realized and rethought over our conversation and made the right decision. It is true that God's Plan of

Salvation is easy. God made it easy so anyone, every one, regardless of age, education, status, gender, or race could simply accept what God has provided.

Sometimes we have to take a step into the unknown. That is what "faith" is all about. Faith is believing in something without having proof of it's validity. No one can prove that God is real. Only when we take that first step of faith toward Him (by believing what He has said to be true) will He (God) prove His reality to us. Without faith we cannot know God personally. One hymn writer puts it in these words.:

> Prayer is the key to heaven, but faith unlocks the door.
> Words are so easily spoken, but prayer without faith
> Is like a boat without an oar.
> So have faith when you speak to the Master
> That's all He asks you for.
> Prayer is the key to heaven, but faith unlocks the door.

So if you want to have a "Precious Jewel" of your own, share your faith and your blessings with someone who needs to come to Christ. When you see that someone, (a child, parent, friend, neighbor, or an acquaintance) pray to receive Christ as their Savior, a chill of happiness (that you never experienced before) will be felt throughout your body. One thing for sure is that there will be great rejoicing in heaven over that lost soul repenting and coming to Christ. (Luke 15:7).

What have I learned by this experience?

Because of this experience, I count it a privilege to be a Child of God and a witness to His presence and blessings. God is in the business of doing only GOOD for those who are His Children and those who have yet to discover His Love for them. It's a good thing to have the weight of evil (Sin) lifted from us, as we strive to live the Christian Life, He (Christ) has promised (John 10;10), via the Holy Spirit's Presence in our lives. I would much prefer looking FORWARD to the more blessed life with Christ, than to always look BACK at the mistakes I've made due to stupidity and lack of direction.

There is JOY in servicing JESUS, as He works in my life and in the lives of those I have had the privilege of introducing to Christ. Only as we are willing to give away what God has given us, can we receive more than we can handle (Malachi 3:10)

> *" 'Bring all the tithes into the storehouse,.*
> *That there may be food in My house,*
> *And proove now in this,'*
> *Says the LORD of hosts,*
> *'If I will not open for you the windows of heaven*
> *And pour out for you such blessing*
> *That there will not be room enough to receive it.'"*

Take heed of the words of a past commercial, "Try it you might like it!" You will never know what I am talking about until you experience it for yourself.

Only one Life, 'Twill soon be past. Only what's done For Christ will last.

Friend

Or Foe?

Chapter Twenty-One

(Jesus said:) "Greater love has no one than this, than to lay down one's life for his friends, You are My friends if you do whatever I command you. No longer do I call you servants, for the servant does not know what his master is doing; but I have called you friends, for all things that I heard from My Father I have made known to you"

John 15:13-15 (N.K.J.)

O NE of the more difficult parts of the Ministry is that one has to be careful about making friends with members of the congregation. One has to be mindful of not showing any sign of favoritism between the members of the church. What makes this so difficult is that human nature tends to gravitate to people of like interests, age and personalities. Being a representative of God, who is no respecter of persons (Acts 10:34), the pastor is expected to give equal time to all who desire his attention. Sometimes the roll of the Pastoral Family can be somewhat lonely, especially for the Pastor's wife. Few if any ever come to visit, just out of friendship.

If any visits are made, it is because of an alternative purpose. The Pastor's wife is expected to be part of all activities, especially with the women's groups, regardless of their age differences. No more should be expected of her than what is expected of any other woman in the church family. The Pastor was the one hired, not the entire Pastoral Family. The pastor's wife is NOT an associate pastor.

When we began our ministry in Michigan, one family in particular took special interest in us. Our son had some health problems when we moved there. This family offered to provide goat's milk and all the eggs we could handle. They lived on what would be considered a small farm. The family consisted of Jay (not his real name), his wife (a nurse at the local hospital), a son, a step-daughter and another young teenager living with them. Another step-son was away serving our country in the armed services. The father, Jay, was known to have some mental health problems. (Don't we all at times?)

When they came to church to worship on Sunday mornings, they sat in the second pew, directly in front of the pulpit. I couldn't miss having eye contact with them, even if I tried (not that I ever wanted to.) Usually at the close of certain hymns, Jay would start to sing the chorus once again, loudly, (sometimes more than once) much to the displeasure of some. The rest of the congregation followed along. (What should a pastor do in such a situation? If you have any suggestions, let me know.)

This family took on the task of mowing the lawn weekly, doing around the parsonage and church, along with the field across the road. One day I called Jay, "Buddy" which upset him greatly. Only homosexuals call each other that", he said. I had never heard that before, maybe he did. Jay and the boys did this task faithfully every week. The County Fair was to be opening soon. The board of trustees decided to give a small check to each of the boys, so they could enjoy the Fair that year. When the father heard this, he became unglued to say the least. He let the board and myself know it, in no uncertain terms, he was not a happy camper. You see he tends to be very controlling in his family. What he says goes.

His step-daughter worked at the local supermarket as a cashier. I didn't dare go to her register to check out. He would become upset. She had to call home when she was ready to go home. He even walked her to her classes at a near by college. Now that's controlling. I only saw her once in church with what I thought to be a boyfriend. Once and only once did that happen.

One summer the family decided to drive to Florida for a vacation. We learned later that when they entered Florida, they had a Van/Truck (18 wheeler) accident. The wife was seriously injured and was in the hospital. Because of the distance involved, I was unable to visit. I called the pastor of one of our denominational churches nearby the hospital. I asked him if he would make a visit on my behalf, which he was more than willing to do. This I believe was the beginning of the end of our friendship. The church family there took great care of them with visits and providing necessary living essentials until they could return home. The church here sent down some funds to help in their return trip home. Other family members used some of the money to travel to Florida, much to the displeasure of Jay.

When they returned home, the wife was admitted to a hospital near by. Being her pastor, I visited her with other members of the church. Jay was not there. He became rather upset that I did it when he was not there. He told me not to return when he was not there. I did a few other times (not by myself), as I felt this is what she wanted. I went to visit her not him. He came to the parsonage and threatened me with physical harm. I was hoping he would not come to church some Sunday, to carry out his threat, which he didn't.

Jay wanted the church to let me go. He told the Board of Deacons that I had interest in his wife. He also said I gave his step-daughter eye contact on Sundays. (How could I not, seeing they sat directly in front of me?). Knowing of his mental health needs, no action was taken.

The step-son, who was in the service, came home and started attending church regularity. A few months later, he asked if I would officiate at his wedding on Christmas Eve. I said I would, much to Jay's displeasure. It was a small wedding with very few of the family members present. The happy couple soon moved away from this area.

It wasn't long soon after, that Jay and his family moved to a new location. They needed a home that was equipped for his wife, seeing she was in a wheelchair. We seldom got to see any of them thereafter, which I am sure was fine with Jay.

A couple of years ago, I did received a phone call from Jay. He was all apollegic for his behavior toward me. He proceeded to let me know that He thought I was doing a good job as Pastor and as a father in raising my son. He did ask for my forgiveness. I told him I was not angry, just a bit disappointed. I told him he was forgiven. I suggested that we meet some day over coffee, if he was ever in the area. That was the last time I spoke with him. Soon after of all this I was notified that he had taken his own life with a shot gun. I suppose he wanted to clean his slat.

His step-daughter soon after gave birth. Jay not only was the grand-father but also the father. She was now free of control and found someone to love her. She got married and had another children. Doing things the right way.

What have I learned from this experience?

The friends we choose help us to become the kind of person we will end up being. Someone once said; "We can only handle ten real good friends at one time." We need to be careful in choosing the people we want around us. The wrong kind will only help us get into trouble of all sorts. The right kind will help us reach our potential in life. The Greatest friend one can have is Jesus Christ. He remains a friend in all kinds of weather and for all eternity. He will never let you down but will help us rise to new and exciting levels in life. "Choose you this day whom you shall serve."

To have Friends
You need to become a Friend.

My Cup's Running Over

Chapter Twenty -two

"You prepare a table before me in the presence of my enemies; You anoint my heard with oil; My cup runs over. Surely goodness and mercy shall follow me all the days of my life; and I will dwell in the house of the Lord forever."

Psalm 23:5,6

T HERE have been blessings received in every part of my living experiences. To list them all would be an endless task here on earth. I enjoy singing the hymn "Count our Blessings". While singing the first stanza, I would sing:

> *"Count your blessings, name them one by one*
> *Count your many blessings , see what God hath done."*

As I sing the second stanza the words change a bit:

> *"Count your blessings, name the two by two,*
> *Count your many blessings, see what God can do."*

I continue to sing the third stanza with the words:

"Count your blessings, weigh them ton by ton,
Count your many blessings, see what God hath done."

Most of my recent blessings have come via my county jail/prison ministry. I had never dreamed of ever wanting to visit or entering such places. It was the last place I ever expected to visit, let alone to minister in. (If the truth be told, I, like most people, could have been one of the residents, had it not been for the Grace of God.)

I have been going "in" and "out" of these correctional facilities for over 20 years, meeting with the inmates on a "person to person" level. There are many Bible Study Groups and Church Services held, but I feel the "one on one" visits are most effective. That is in my experience. I can get these men and women to face up to their personal problems with the law and society. This would be a bit difficult to do with other people around.

I have met with inmates from all walks of life, all ages, both genders, various occupations (or lack thereof), varied educational opportunities (some can neither read nor write - YES, here in America), singles, married, divorced, religious and non-religious. You name it and they can be found incarcerated somewhere. You can read more from my previous book: "The Key to Freedom from Captivity " published by: w.w.w.AuthorHouse.com. I have a second book like this waiting to be completed and published. It is entitled: "Exist in Darkness - Live in The Light". It is five small books in one - Jailhouse Poetry, Jailhouse Artistry, Jailhouse Registry, Jailhouse Testimonies, and Jailhouse Activities.

There have been hundreds of decisions made to receive Jesus Christ as Savior over these many years. Many of these men/women have long since been released after serving their time. I have tried to keep in touch with as many as I could, for follow-up work, but was successful to only a few. I did what I could (planting the seed of Salvation). Now I have to turn them over to the Holy Spirit to do the follow-up. Mentioned below are a few that I still have contact with.

* * * * * * * * * * * * * * * * * * * *

Let us first make mention of "J.W." He was arrested in his early twenties. He accepted Christ as his Savior while residing at the county jail. He was sentenced to over 10 years in the state facilities. He served his time well, leaving there without any bitterness or anger. He acknowledged his error in judgment and willingly paid the price. Recently he was released and was able to find employment in the field he is most interested in, the medical field. While working he is taking the necessary classes to advance. This is not the norm for most inmates who are released. He is a very contented man at present and looking forward to becoming married and purchasing his own home and starting a family. His desire is to become a meaningful asset to society. He has learned and acknowledges that he is both an important and Special person. He is on his way to becoming the person God created him to be.

* * * * * * * * * * * * * * * * * * * *

Let us now look at A.F. When I got to meet him, he was being housed in the county jail from another county. He was in his early twenties. His was a serious crime (C.S.C. - Criminal Sexual Conduct). He had little if any family life to speak of. He was molested by all his family while an infant and this became a way of life for all involved. He decided while we met to become a member of the Family of God, a new experience for him. He learned what family-life could and should be like. He had a jury trial and was found guilty. His guidelines called for a sentence of 7 - 15 years. The presiding judge, desiring to make an example of him, exceeded the guidelines and sentenced him to 60 - 90 years. We have kept in touch over the years. I more or less became a father figure to him. He has kept hold of his faith in Christ, under I am sure most difficult circumstances. He could only be doing this by the Grace of God, as the apostle Paul found out when God told him: *"My grace is sufficient for you, for My strength is made perfect in weakness..." (II Corinthians 12:9).* God can and will use anyone of us, wherever we find ourselves, for His purposes.

* *

Let us look next at a young man we'll call "J.L.". As a result of his crime, he ended up having serious family problems. He ended up having to give up his parental rights, I believe because of his incarceration. I was able to be with him when this took place in the court. We do keep in touch, writing to each other and occasional visits. He is regretful for his past life and is presently seeking to reform. His goal is to keep his life clean and become a useful citizen of society when he is released in a couple of years. Only his faith in Christ has kept him from becoming bitter and revengeful. He clings to the words of his Savior and Lord, Jesus Christ *"Beloved, do not avenge yourself, but rather give place to wrath; for it is written, 'Vengeance is Mine, I will repay,' says the Lord."* *(Romans 112:19)*

* * * * * * * * * * * * * * * * * * * *

S.M. is another young man who was arrested along with his brother for stealing a snowmobile. They were also into drugs and alcohol. They did not go to prison but served their time in the county jail. Since their release a number of years ago, S.M. has been attempting to get his life on the right path. He has kept himself free of drugs and alcohol as far as I can observe. He is a multi-talented person. Presently , he is attempting to start up a business using his many talents, especially in the construction line. Working along side of him is a young lady, whom he is living with. They have a beautiful daughter together. Now to only get them married, that is my goal. Satan has not been making life easy for them. He could have turned back to drugs, a life more livable, but has chosen to keep on the straight and narrow, which is more difficult. He knows well that he cannot do this on his own. He realizes his need of Christ and the Holy Spirit in his life every day. I know that if he remains faithful to his God and his faith in Christ, he will eventually have the victory that he is seeking.

* *

C.B. is another young man I had met, He was working with and for S.M. doing construction. He later was charged with driving while drinking (D.U.I. - Driving under the influence), which of course is a No! No!. He was placed in the county jail until his arraignment. I visited with him there and told him of God's Love for him and that with God's help, he could win over alcohol. He informed me, as of this writing, that he hasn't had a drink for over a year. He was placed on probation for a few years and lost the used of his driver's license for a few years.

* *

T.C. is another young man who was arrested along with his friend C.A. Both were involved with under-aged girls, (claiming to be much older) seeking physical, sexual pleasure. Both were tried in court and found guilty of the crime they were charged with, and served time in the county jail and state correctional facilities. Both these young men received Christ as their Savior as they became aware of the love God has for them I did have the opportunity to visit with each, at different facilities, the years that followed. Both took great interest in the Bible Study groups and church services that were provided. Both are now married and they hardly see each other any more. T.C., I know has been living a good, lawful life with his family. C.A. has found life to be more difficult. I have little contact with C.A. at the present time. Not everything works out the way we would like, especially if we try to go it alone. One day my wife and I was having lunch at a local restaurant and a man approached me and asked if I remembered him. He looked familiar, but I could not remember his name. He gave a few glues and I finally got his name. It was T.C. He was there with his wife. All was going well with him. He thanked me for introducing him to Christ. And being his friend.

* *

The other day as I was checking out at the local supermarket, I noticed a young man waving to get my attention. After checking out, I approached him. He sure enough knew me, but I could not recognize him, but I pretended that I did. Sure enough it was a young man I had visited while he was in the county jail. There have been far too many for me to remember them all. He told me he was doing well and was planning on getting married. He was working and things seemed well with him. I told him of my published book and showed him one that was in the store. He said he was going to purchase one. I'm still not sure who he is, but that doesn't really matter. He remembered me and that alone made my day. God knows who he is, that's all that really matters.

* * * * * * * * * * * * * * * * * * * *

One day as I was entering the local supermarket, I noticed another young man I had never met before. What was outstanding was his appearance. It was a cold, wintery, rainy day. He was attempting to make a phone call. He was dressed in a white tee shirt and pants. He had only socks on his feet with no shoes. (The sheriff's office released him with the same things he was arrested with. What he came in with, he left with and nothing more.)   I did my shopping and as I was leaving, he was still outside, trying to make the call. I approached him. I thought for sure he was just released from the county jail, not too far from there. He told me he was trying to get a ride to Osseo, a couple of miles down the road.

I offered him a lift, as I had some time to spare. I first took him to the local Salvation Army Store. There he was able to find a shirt, a warm coat and shoes. They offered them to me free of charge, seeing I was a pastor. I drove him to Osseo and his home. I gave him some literature I had in the car. We parted company at this point. I later saw him in one of the fast food establishments. He remembered me right off and thanked me once again for the kindness I showed. I only know him today as Tony. I hope he got to read the material I left with him.

* * * * * * * * * * * * * * * * * * * *

I could go on and on, as I have done in my book, I mentioned earlier. These and many, many more, have been my richest blessings.

There is no greater Joy one can receive than to introduce another to the Love of God, through Jesus Christ and see them turn their lives over to Him. Herein lies my Joy, Happiness and Blessings. As the title of a hymn puts it: "There is Joy in Serving Jesus."

What I have learned by these experiences?

A good deed will never goes unnoticed in God's eyes. We may not see the final results immediately, but somewhere along the line, it will bear fruit. The scripture says it best: *"Who receives you receives Me, (Christ) and he who receives Me receives Him who sent Me. He who receives a prophet in the name of a prophet shall receive a prophet's reward. And he who receives a righteous man in the name of a righteous man shall receive a righteous man's reward. And whoever gives one of these little ones only a coup of cold water in the name of a disciple, assuredly, I say to you, he shall by no means lose his reward." (Matthew 10:40-42)*

Don't let your Past
be an excuse for your Future

Hurry Up
and
Wait

Chapter Twenty-Three

"Those who wait on the LORD shall renew their strength; They shall mount up with wings like eagles, they shall run and not be weary, they shall walk and not faint."

Isaiah 40:31

WAITING has never been one of my favorite past-times. I am a very impatient person when I'm called upon to wait for anything. Time to me is a most valuable commodity and should not be wasted needlessly. Once time has gone it is gone forever and cannot be reclaimed or relived. .

When I was a high school student, I felt called into full-time Christian Service, while attending a Christian Endeavor Conference (Chapter Nine - "Eleven-Eleven-Eleven"). I had to wait two years before I could begin my preparation for entering college. It took another five years to complete my college education for ministry.

Not being able to enter seminary as I had hoped, I found it necessary to find secular employment, in order to provide a living for my family. It was during this time I had to learn how to wait patiently. I had to wait every day as I went to work in Boston. I had to wait in all kinds of New England weather for public transportation, only to see the buses pass me by, being filled to capacity, thus having to wait for the next bus to arrive. This went on day after day, week after week, month after month, year after year, much to my frustration. This all meant I had to leave earlier than the distance required and to get home later than desired. The automobile was not an option for me or my family. My father never owned or drove an automobile in all his life. I didn't learn to drive until I was in my early twenties.

People who found themselves in the same predicament as I, knowing they were going to have to wait, brought with them a book or newspaper to read while waiting. No matter where they went or what mode of transportation they were going to use, they knew for certain there was going to be a waiting time.

It was in the year 1953 that I graduated from high school, after which I entered Gordon College of Theology and Missions, then located in Boston MA., now located in Wenham, MA. Two years after I started college, I transferred to the New England School of Theology in Brookline, MA to complete my college education, receiving a B.A. in Theology Degree in 1958. This was another year longer then most people spend in college.

Another period of waiting took place. It took another twenty years after graduation before I finally got to be ordained as a Minister of the Gospel on May, 1981, as I pastored my first pastorate of two churches in the state of Pennsylvania. I found it difficult at times and exasperating trying to understand why God made me "wait" twenty years to began. I suppose it could have been I needed time to become more mature for the ministry He had in mind for me. I learned we aren't always to fully understand God's ways. They are not always the same as our ways. Someone once said, "God may not always be on time (our time that is) , but He is never late.(His timing)"

It was during my second pastorate I was introduced to the art of waiting once again. According to one family, I was not doing my ministry to their satisfaction or fulfilling my contract with them in their eyes. (What contract? I thought I was workiing for God not man.) They in turn so manipulated the funds of the church, the church stopped payments of my medical insurance and retirement account, in hopes that I would seek to minister elsewhere. I prayed and turned this situation over to God, seeking a new pastorate. I waited a full year and God did not respond as I had hoped. (Sometimes God makes us wait for His timing.) The family that was unappreciative of my ministry again rearranged the funds of the church. I was informed that my salary had to be cut in half, due to the lack of money in the general account. God and I went back into discussion. I looked into a number of possibilities from Maine, along the east coast and Pennsylvania, but none opened. Another year went by working with half a paycheck. My not moving displeased the family mentioned earlier. Most of the money received by the church was placed into a building fund, which was not needed. The church asked me to preach on Sundays and I would be allowed to stay at the parsonage as my pay. (No pay check) I waited another year before God decided to move me to Michigan. The unhappy family decided to move to a new church long before I got to move, as they had hoped. God has His way of dealing with people of conflict to His plans.

I could not understand why God did not act sooner. Only years later as I looked back, did I began to see God's Plan. He was preparing me for the Jail/Prison Ministry I have in Michigan in addition to my church ministry. He also was preparing the church in Hillsdale to accept me and His plans for Hillsdale.

Recently I found myself in another period of having to wait. This came after I had retired at the age of 67. I made myself available to my denomination to serve as an Interim Pastor. Shortly after I purchased my home, I was asked to go to eastern PA to serve church there as Interim. I was there for one year and moved back to Hillsdale. I prayed for another open door after that. It has been now nearly four years with no open door. I sure wish I were tuned into God's Plan for my family and I. All I can do is pray and wait once again.

The one good thing that I have been able to accomplish while waiting is the writing and publishing my first book on the Jail Ministry "The Key to Freedom from Captivity". I wrote another book, a sequel the first "Exist in Darkness - LIVE in the Light". The book you are now reading is another of my endeavors. I trust you have enjoyed it as much as I reminisced and recorded these memories.

What have I learned by this experience?

Even though I have no insight as to what the future may hold, I am thankful I have confidence in the One who hold my future. At present I may not know the reason behind all of my waiting, I am assured that it will become clear as time goes on. God says: *"Now we see in a mirror, dimly, but then face to face. Now I know in part, but then I shall know just as I also am known."*
(I Corinthians 13:12.)

God has promised to answer ALL of the prayers of His children. It sometimes is "YES" and we receive what we have asked for. At other times the answer is "NO". What we have asked for is not for our benefit at that time. God has something far better in mind for us. We sometimes have to accept the answer "WAIT" for a more suitable time and place for the fulfillment of our request. We have to accept that the answer is not always "YES" or immediate, but an answer will come eventually, at God's timing and in Hid place of service.

We make a Living by what we get
We make a Life by what we give.

My Brother's Keeper

Chapter Twenty-Four

"My God shall supply all your needs according to His riches in glory by Christ Jesus"

Philippians 4:19

"The Lord is my shepherd, I shall not want...(He) anoints my head with oil; My cup runs over..."

Psalm 23:1,5b

"Now to Him who is able to do exceedingly abundantly above all that we ask or think, according to the power tht works in us. To Him be glroy in the church by Christ Jesus..."

Ephesians 3:20,21a.

I COULD not have accomplished all that I have without the friendship, fellowship and companionship of my many fellow-clergy. Pastors are encouraged not to become too friendly with members of the congregation they are serving. Often times this causes times of loneliness for the First Family of the church. While church families are able to gather for various family activities (birthdays, anniversaries, weddings, reunions and the like) the Pastoral Family is usually miles away from their family members, only to see them while on vacation time. It takes many months for a new family to acclimate to new surroundings, sometimes never happening.

I have dedicated this book to only a few of our closest friends in ministry. As I bring this book to a close, I would like to say "Thank You" to all who have helped to make my ministry as a Pastor as successful as it has become. Some stand out more in my memory than do others due to our close relationships. That is not to say that the others have been forgotten, by any means, in the role they played in my life over the years. Let me take time to recognize only a few who have become near and dear to my family. These were at one time or other my pastors.

REV. GORDON JAMES KIRK was the first to make a lasting impression on my young life. Growing up, he became a Father figure to me. Through his ministry I came to know, love, and accept Jesus Christ as my Personal Savior. We worked many hours and years together, working to get the church weekly bulletin printed on the old, now obsolete mimeograph machine, if anyone remembers them, They are very messy when in use. His home become my second home. I was either there or at the church if my family needed to get in touch with me. Mrs. Doris Kirk, his wife had a great voice and was able to sing, "I'd Rather Have Jesus" at my ordination recognition service in 1981.His son, Richard was part of my youth group. Today Richard is serving a yoke ministry (two church at the same time.) in Pennsylvania. This family has made a definite attachment in my life.

DR. MORRIS ALTON INCH became my Pastor after leaving a church in South Boston, Massachusetts. He and his wife Joan worked as partners on many various programs during his ministry with us. Their children became very close to me and my family. One in particular seemed to bond with me for some reason, Thomas.

Today Tom is serving as a pastor of a Lutheran Church in the state or Washington. Pastor Inch conducted a week's conference for the Christian Endeavor Movement in Northfield, MA. It was during this conference that I dedicated my life to full-time Christian Service. I was a junior in high school at the time.(Chapter nine, "Eleven, Eleven, Eleven" pages 53-57) . After leaving the pastorate, he become the Dean at Wheaton College in Illinois for a number of years, until he took up a teaching role in a college in Jerusalem, Israel. He is presently retired, he became an author writing many books on his religious beliefs. It was during his ministry I was granted a license to preach by the church and later certified by the state denominational convention on November 24, 1968.

REV. FREDERICK NAGLE became an associate pastor working under Pastor Inch. He later became pastor of the West Somerville Baptist Church. As time went on, his church and two others joined forces (because of low attendance) and formed a new church, the Somerville Community Baptist Church. I was on the committee that established this church. Fred and I worked hand and hand and I became a chaplain, working with the nursing homes and hospital within the city. Whenever I made a fast trip back east, Pastor Nagle made sure I was given the opportunity to preach, receiving not only the normal honorarium but added more for traveling. He later retired and is now living in Florida..We have been in contact since his retirement, over the phone. Recently Fred departed to receive his Heavenly Reward late in 2009.

REV. THOM BLACK became my pastor, moving from the state of Maine where he was serving three churches at the same time. You might say I was responsible for him coming south. Thom is an Irishmen and one has to either like the man, or they will find him hard to really like. He quickly recognized my calling to the ministry. I was then working for Converse Rubber, selling seconds athletic shoes. He told me one day, "You don't belong behind the counter selling soles. You are suppose to be in the pulpit saving souls." He further informed me that I was going to get ordained, whether I liked it or not. He was going to make sure. He did everything within his power to make this a reality. This he did and here I am. He became a pastor of another church in Michigan until he retired to Louisiana to be close to some of his children. He lived there a number of years until hurricane Katrina hit the Gulf coast. Along with many others, his home was destroyed and he moved to Ohio to be close to others of his children. He has built a new home there. Thom and his wife Doris were able to move into their new home a few months ago. I received one of those midnight phone calls that no one wishes to receive. It was on Wednesday, October10, 2007 that Doris, his wife, called to inform me that Thom had been transported to his new heavenly abode that Christ had prepared for him (John 14:1,2) His kidneys failed and before getting on dialysis Thom raised his hands above his head and said, "You better hurry up because I am going home." (And he did). I know he heard the words, "Well done thou good and faithful servant..." from the God he proclaimed for many years in ministry.

REV. GEORGE URBAN was more than a pastor to me. He pastored my church for only a few years. During that time we became close friends. We lost contact with each other for a number of years. He had since retired and I later discovered he was living in Arkansas. A few years back we renewed our friendship when he heard my being honored on radio, I was featured on the "Unshackled" program from Chicago. Illinois. (Chapter 12 - "Across the Waves"). He contacted me and we picked up where we left off many years earlier. We have been in contact since via the E-mail.

DR. RICHARD ECKLEY became a close friend while I was serving a church in Bentleyville, PA. He became pastor of the Wesleyan Church. He was a young pastor with great expectations. We worked well together over the years he was there. He was new to the ministry and looked to me for help. We call each other "father and son" because one day I drove him to Pittsburgh, PA to have some dental work done in one of the hospitals. One of the nurses asked if Rich was my son. I was told then that my son would soon be done. Every since them we call each other dad and son. We have fun with this so-called relationship, even though we are brothers in Christ. He left the church in PA and began working at the Houghton College in New York. We have carried on that relationship ever since. He has since became a full professor there. He received his Doctorate and is now a full professor at the college. He has recently published a book, a commentary on the biblical book of Revelation. That makes him an author as well.

I could go on and on but space will not allow it. I had to pick and choose from my many clergy family. I choose only those who pastored me over the years. I apologize to all the others who are my brothers and sisters in ministry. There are many others who have assisted me and my family in ministry for which I am deeply grateful.

On one occasion when my family and I were having difficulties, while we were meeting at a local fast food restaurant, it was suggested that they pray for my situation. Yes, we had a Prayer Meeting in the middle of a restaurant. As a result of that prayer time, a fellow pastor, who also was a farmer, asked if we could use some meat. He later delivered to our home, box after box of cuts of meat, totaling a half of a cow. It was enough to fill our freezer. Isn't it great how God keeps His promise to provide for all our needs? Unfortunately a few years later he was a victim of a farm accident and was called to his eternal abode. Someone once said, "God's work, done God's way will never lack God's supply."

God promises
a safe landing
not a calm passage

The
Listening
Post

Chapter Twenty-Five

" ...Take heed what you hear (listen to). With the same measure you use, it will be measured to you; and to you who hear (listen), more will be given. "

Mark 4:24 (KJV)

T HERE are many places in history and in the present where we find the word "Post" mentioned. In the early days of the growth of our nation, while dealing with the Indian tribes, there were the "Trading Posts". Here is where we see the barter system operating. This is where Indians would bring in their furs, jewelry and the likes to trade for food and necessary items. Today one can find only a few Indian Trading Posts. Cash is the currency needed for purchases.

The "Post-script" was and is used by those who wrote letters, when writing letters, was the main means of communication. After a letter had been completed, an after thought might come to mind and needed to be included. Rather than redoing the complete letter a (P.S. - Postscript) would be added, after the signature. This could be an answer to a question previously asked, added information that just came to mind, or a clearer explanation of subject matter. This is rarely used today because of the new form of reaching people with the E-mail, I-mail, which is a much faster and cheaper means of communication with each other.

The Saturday Evening POST, a magazine published a few years ago when there were many fewer magazines on the market. It was a family type publication with many interesting pictures from around the world, covering current events. It was not for a selective group of people, as many are today. Many of Norman Rockwell's paintings were featured on the cover.

There is also the ever faithful "POST Office"where nothing would ever prevent the delivery of the mail, neither snow, sleet, rain or any other natural force would keep them for their appointed task. It started out with the "Pony Express" during the nation's early growth to the present "Priority Mail" today. I use to be able to mail a letter for 3 cents per letter. Now with the many increases, that same letter would cost me 44 cents to send. With the new focus on electronic mailing (e-mail) regular mailing is now known as "Snail-mail", unless you are willing to pay dearly to have over-night delivery. (Priority Mailing.

The Hitching POST is another one of those things in history. It was when a person came into town to purchase things, they would tie their horses to a "hitching POST" while they went about their business. Today we have gone from a one or two horse-power means of transportation, to hundreds of horse-power vehicles. In place of the hitching post, we now have driveways and garages to park our many horse-powered means of transportation. Some churches have been called a "Hitching POSTS" when people decide to get "Hitched" (Married that is).

The purpose for this chapter is not just to reminisce about the past as it might seem at this point. I became acquainted with another "POST" a few years ago. It is one that I had never heard of but soon after experienced first hand.

It all started while I was serving as an Interim Pastor in Factoryville, PA at the turn of the century. Close to my place of ministry stood the Keystone College, almost walking distance from the church. While a few of the pastors were meeting one day, we were talking about the importance of "listening" in our field of service. Listening is the key to effective ministry, be it clergy or lay people. God has given all of us a ministry to perform, wherever we find ourselves. We through around the idea of establishing what we called a "Listening Post" at the college, if we could obtain permission. It took a while, but after many meetings with the college president and officers, it was agreed to give it a trial run.

The "Listening Post" was not to be a religious movement in any respect, although it was maned by ministers mainly, both male and female pastors from the various denominations. We simply found a area in the college where the students usually gathered. We agreed to set up shop near the cafeteria and mail boxes. Both were conveniently located close to each other. We set up a few soft chairs and a sofa. The cafeteria supplied us with fruit or snacks. It was decided to hold the "Listening Post" twice a week, one during the noon hour and one during the dinner hour. Each pastor would take turns, so as not to let it become a burden to any. We posted a sign near by "The Listening Post", which became sort of a drawing card to get some attention from the students.

The purpose of the "Listing Post" was simply to make ourselves available to the students who needed someone to talk to. We were there primarily to "Listen" to whatever the students had to say. At first it was talk about why we were there and to satisfy their curiosity.

I can only write of my experiences with this program. Unfortunately my participation only lasted a few months before I ended my pastorate in Factoryville. As short as my time there was, I considered the effort made, to be a successful endeavor.

One afternoon waiting for somebody, anybody to stop by for a time of conversation, a young man stopped. It was obvious that he was a foreign student. We introduced ourselves to break the ice. For the purpose of this book I'll give him the name of Al.

Al began by telling me he hadn't been in America but for a short while. He had only been at Keystone College a few months. It was his first time away from his home in India and was homesick to say the least. I encouraged him to tell me about his family and country. He told me a bit of his religion (Moslem) and I shared my faith with him. We must have talked about an hour or so. He became more relaxed and comfortable. Before leaving he expressed his appreciation for our talk. He said, talking with me reminded him of his talks with his grandfather (he could have left off the word "grand" and that would have suited me fine.) I returned home that evening feeling pretty good and felt it was time well spent. Leaving the area shortly thereafter, I was unable to keep in touch with Al, the sad part of this experience.

Because of my moving back to Michigan, my connection with the "Listening POST was short lived. I would love to be able to get another "Listening POST" started at Hillsdale College someday. I think at present it would be a task most difficult to accomplish. They have a catholic priest serving as a chaplain and he has his own program. I haven't given up that this project.It might happen sometime in the future.

What have I learned by this experience?

God has given us two ears and only one mouth. This tells me we should be *listening* twice as much as we speak. It is so easy for us to put forth our own agenda when speaking to people. If we take the time to *listen*, we might be able to see the best way to help another person, who is troubled.

Physiologist endeavor to get their client to speak while they listen. If a person opens-up to someone they trust, generally speaking, a person is able to solve their own problem. They just need someone to become a sounding board. Once they see the problem in front of them, they are able to work out a solution on their own

We all have problems and solutions are not always easy to find. Remember, to never forget, that there is One we can turn to that has ALL the answers. Jesus Christ, our Lord and Savior, is His name.

Aspire to Inspire, Before you Expire.

Sweet
and
Sour

Joy
and
Sadness

Chapter Twenty-Six

ONE of the more difficulties in the role of a Pastor has to do with one's emotions. You might say that the Pastor has to be all things for all people. When there is a wedding to officiate at, he has to be happy or at least wear the happy face. When there is a funeral to conduct, sadness is the rule for the day for the sake of the family members. When there is a birth or addition to the family, one has to display a joyful appearance for all concerned. This is a most difficult task as anyone can imagine.

What makes these various experineces more difficult is when one or more events occur close together, even days or hours between. It is most diffcult to turn one's emotions on and off with little time between the events. It becomes even harder especially when those involved are slightly known or yet even strangers. Recently these experiences became a reality when it involves not strangers, friends, or church members but one of one's own biological family.

It was on May 28, 2008 that I was invited to my bother's 50th Wedding Anniversary in Cape Cod, MA. It involved having to travel over 1000 miles, with gas prices out of sight. I discovered that my wife, son and I could fly cheaper and faster than to try to drive the distant, and far less tiring.

We looked forward to this time of getting together for this landmark event in the family. We never had gotten together for a family reunion. Not many get to celebrate an important achievement in these days.

My brother is two years older then myself. We have had many and varied experiences over the years. I looked forward to sharing this happy time with he and his wife.

My brother and I were diognosed with Prostate Canser some 12 years ago. I had surgery and his was inoperable. We celebrated the fact that we outlived many of our friends, who had simular health conditions to live with. The past years were less kind to him during this time than it was for me. He had to attend this joyous event in a wheelchair, but nonetheless he was able to participate in this milestone event beside his wife and their family. There were few times when our family were able to gather together. This made it even more meanningful for those who did attend.

It proved to be costly when all was said and done, but when it comes to family one does not count the cost, as we discovered later. We returned home, happy to have made the trip.

It was only a month later I received a call from my niece, my brother's daughter, informing me that her dad, my brother, had passed away due to his cancer. What was once a time of happiness had now turned to be a time of sadness. .

What made things more difficult is that I was asked by my sister-in-law if I would officiate at the funeral service. Without hesitation I consented to do so. I have been asked by some, how I, as a pastor, could conduct so many funerals and not become affected. The reason is because we can sort of emotionally remove ourselves from becoming persoanlly connected and forcus on the service itself and minister to those who are huarting. When one does become personally involved, emotions have a way of making things difficult.

I had to fly back to Cape Cod by myself this time because of the shortness of time and the added expenses involved. This was not going to be the joyous event as was my previous trip. My joy had now turned into sadness. The sweetness of the month before had now turned sour, in a manner of speaking. The gladness had turned into sadness.

In order to conduct the service I had to make this one like any other that I had conducted in the past. I remained outside of the room the service was to be in and made sure that the casket was behind me, out of eye contact. All went well until I had to mention my brother's name and that was when things become personal. I had to stop speaking momentarily to regain my composure. I got through it and truly glad I was called upon to do my part.

My brother was an addent fisherman. Most of his life on the Cape was spending his time with his friends or alone in a boat somewhere in the Atlantic Ocean. This was who he was and what he lived to do. He even operated a Bat & Tackle business, which he later turned over to one of his sons. You might say we had this somewhat in common. He was the "fisherman" of the family and I became a "Fisher-of-men" for the cause of Christ.

We now have only our memories to draw upon, with gladness and with sadness.This in one way he contnues to live as a family member. He was cremated and his remains were placed where he had spent a good portion of his life, in his favorite fishing spots, in and around Buzzards Bay, MA.

What have I learned by this e xperience?

This like so many other things that happen in life teaches us that life on earth is but a short period of time. Life is like a vapor that once is and that is no more. In eternity one day on earth is likened to a thousand years in heaven. One never knows from one day to the next if there is going to be another day to be about our Father's business. Whatever we need to do or say needs to be done today, because when that final tomorrow arrives, our work on earth will end. "Only one life, 'twill soon be past. Only what's done for Christ will last." What will be left behind when we leave this earth that will tell people who we were and what we have done?

New Lease
On Life

Chapter Twenty-Seven

Jesus said, "...I am come that they may have life and that they may have it more aboundantly."

John 10:10

WHEN we first came to Michigan one of our first things to accomplish was to find a doctor in the community. It was suggested we get in touch with a Doctor/Surgeon who was accepting new patients. He was well respected and was considered the best in his field. He served us well over the years. Our first major encounter was when our son put his hand under a running lawn mower to release a rock that had stopped the mower, not realizing it was still running. Fortunately he was wearing gloves. He washed off the finger under the outside water faucet and came into the house asking for a bandade. My wife was at the church for a ladies' supper. I had to rush him to the hospital and the doctor had to reconstruct his finger which took hours. Fortunately he was able to save the finger and only lost the tip of it.

As time went on the doctor found it was about time he retired from practice and moved out of the area. His replacment was a young an who was strickly a Family Practitioner. I became his first patient as it turned out. Getting to know my medical history he sent me to have a complete blood work done. Thank God I had the necessary insurance to cover all he desired. I guess it's better to be safe than to get into difficulty later down the road.

You might say he was giving me an "Organ Recital." He was going to check out my lungs, my liver, my kidneys, my blood pressure, and my chamical balance. He checked out the medication I was taking and made the changes he thought necessary. After all was said and done; I ended up having at this time an EKG (for the heart), a CAT-scan, which I couldn't have (they couldn't slow down my heart beat enough.), an ECHO scan (sound waves) instead and a colonostophy which came out negative. Finally he did all he could think of but said that I needed to have my heart looked at. He arranged to have me meet with a cardiologist. Another CAT-scan was ordered. This time things worked out and he was able to get a reading of my heart's condition. He discovered that I had a slight blockage in one of the arteries. He made the necessary arrangements to have me go to the Borgess Medical Center in Kalamazoo, MI (abut 85 mmiles away) to have a stent implanted if necessary. This is a common occurance these days. I had no indication that anything was wrong with my heart. I felt good.

Seeing the appintment was at 6:00 in the morning, my wife and son accompanied me in going to Kalamazoo the night before, rather than leaving so early in the morning. We didn't bring much clothing because we expected to be returning home the same day.

After they got started they decided not to use a stent or anything else for that matter. I was told that what I needed was an open-heart surgery. One of the major arteries that fed the other arteries was just about completely blocked. I needed by-pass surgery. Later (thank God it was later and not before) I was told that this was considered to be a "Widow-maker". Any type of attack could have taken my life at any moment, if not treated. There would have been no time to revive me.

Surgery was set for the following week, due to the busy schedule. My wife and son returned home and waited for the day of surgery.

I spent six days alone, but I was not really alone, God was there with me. They returned to spend time time with me after the surgery. They were able to stay at the Hospitality House near-by free of expenses. Even then the surgery was delayed for a day.

On the day of surgery, I was moved from the first floor (short stay unit) to the fifth to be readied and after to the eight floor after recovery. Here I spent the next five days until my release. In addition the 15 inch incision made in my chest I had also three 6 inch incisions in my legs where they took veins to put into the heart area (A triple by-pass). After I was released I had a visiting nurse come to the house twice a week for about a month. All involved were amazed at the rapid healing that took place, seeing I am a diabedic.

The only real pain I endured was when I had to caugh. That was almost unbearable at times. I was given a friend to help me with the pain. It was a stuffed Moose which I held to my chest and squeezed as hard as I could when I caughed. It was truly my "Caughing Buddy". I suspect he will be a friend and a reminder of what a friend aught to be.

The only other problem I encountered was what I feared most. I became a bit bound-up, as a side effect of the pain medication I had to take from time to time. I feared it becasue I had a similar experience once before when I spent eight hours in the emergency room. I never drank so much prune juice as I did to help releave the problem. I know I didn't dare apply much pressure. With God's help in due time I did move and found great relief. Just one of those things we deal with in life. Not everything is pleasant.

After returning home, one of my friends. A poet in her own rights woke up early and had me on her mind. She penned a poem with me in mind, the words of which are these:

Different But Wholesome

This Christmas,

Because of illness,
I'm slowed down,
I won't decorate.

I will not
Mail out a lot of
Christmas cards
Or bake lots of stuff.

But I'll know
My limitations,
And wisely
Halt expectations.

But my heart
Will sing Christmas songs.
Jesus Christ's
There, where He belongs.

molly a. marsh
17, December 2008
4:49 a.m.

What have I learend by this experience?

Do not take your health for granted. Even when everything seems to be right, something major could be happening. Keep your physical exams done on a regular basis. The smallest thing coud be a sign of something dangerous.

Take life serious and use the time you have to the fullest, one day at a time. Life is like a burning candle. You never know when or how quickly the flame may become extinguished and become useless.

The Major lesson I have learned and am reminded of is that God is still in charge. He is still on the throne directing and seeing that His will, will be done in each of our lives. God knows when and how much we are hurting. At His timing not ours, He puts all things in place and does what needs to happen.

God knew my condition before anyone else and He chose the time to set things right. That's what He did in my case. At His timing I was given not only a New Life in Christ but now a New Lease on Life. Now I can begin a New Year with a New outlook and modivaton to live life to the fullest.

Closing
Thoughts

"If we [freely] admit that we have sinned and confess our sins, He is faithful and just [true to His own nature and promises] and will forgive our sins (dismiss our lawlessness) and continuously cleanse us from all unrighteousness - everything not in conformity to His will in purpose, thought and action."

I John 1:9 (Amplified)

As I bring this book to a close, I hope, as I have reflected back over my journey through life, you have received some sort of a blessing. Perhaps it has given you an opportunity to do some reflecting of your own.

This was not meant to be an autobiography. My intention is to show that "Pastors" are not superhuman or exempt from the ups and downs of a person's life. We are merely human beings, like yourself, who have been called to serve God and mankind with the spiritual gifts God has given us.

Pastors are sometimes called "Ministers" or "preachers" along with other names (good names of course). All of God's children (those who have received Jesus Christ as Savior) are called to "minister" in their special field of service, using the spiritual gifts that God has given them. We just have to discover the What, the Where and Way God desires us to minister. To be called, set apart and sanctified is to be ordained by God, Himself. Have YOU found your place of ministry?

As the saying goes: "all pictures have a story to tell", so every person has a purpose, a mission and a special calling. Every life has a story to reveal. All we have to do is let it loose and share what God has done, is doing and will accomplish through us.

I have discovered as I have listened to the various stories of other people, they open to us the treasure chests we tend to keep hidden. As the words of the song says: "It is no secret what God can do, What He's done for others He can do for you."

It is true that there are parts of our lives that should remain private, things known only to us and to God. Nevertheless, what God has done through our experiences could possibly help others as they face similar circumstances

We taught our children from childhood how important it is to share what we have with others. This might be the time for us to start practicing what we preached. Only good can come, when we share experiences with one another.

We all have received, I am confident, many blessings (if we take the time to consider them) over many years. Blessings do come from God, but they are not meant to be kept to ourselves. To receive the full impact of a blessing, it needs to be shared, passed on to others. Then and only then can we experience the full potential of a blessing. Freely we have received God's blessings, so let us freely give (share) them with someone else.

If you have not yet received what you consider to be a blessing from God (That is most unlikely), it's about time to think about giving yourself (your control) over to Him. Turn you life over to Him by receiving Jesus Christ as our personal Savior. He gave His life in order that you might live forever as a child of God. Just confess your sin and sinful nature and ask for His forgiveness. (Read the scripture at the beginning of this chapter).

You simply need to repeat the following prayer of repentance, Don't do it just because I have suggested it. It needs to come from the heart and not just the lips. Be assured, God knows where is coming from. If it is sincere, God will forgive your sinful past and give you a new start in life. A new page in the book you are writing as you live. Immediately you will become His child and He will give you the presence of the Holy Spirit to guide your daily walk.

Dear God:

I do believe that you created me and You do love me. I believe You have a purpose for my being alive. I realize I have done much that has been displeasing to You. That make me what the Bible calls a sinner. and deserving of eternal death. Please forgive and cleanse me from my sin and sinful nature. I do believe that Jesus Christ died in my place, in order that I might become Your child. I now accept Christ as my personal Savior and Lord. Thanks for accepting me as you child.

A- men

A Wishbone cannot replace a Backbone

Pastors are not any different then those of their congregations, We are ordinary human beings fulfilling the Calling we received from God. I have served over 50 years in ministry, recognized by the Am. Bapt, Chs./ U.S.A. I was ordained in May, 1981, serving seven churches throughout this country. For 20 years plus, my jail/prison ministry has helped hundreds of inmates individually. I am part of the certified C.I.S.M. (Critical Incident Stress Management) team in Hillsdale, MI. Educational qualifacations consist of High School, attending

Gordon College, and Berkshire Christian College, receiving a B A. degree in Theology. Married Norma Lee (Newton) and we have one son, Mark Kenneth. My first published book, "The Key to Freedom from Captivity" (2003).